Aladdin

A pantomime

David Cregan

Music by
Brian Protheroe

Samuel French — London
New York - Toronto - Hollywood

ISBN 0 573 16404 5

ALADDIN

First presented at the Theatre Royal, Stratford East on 30th November 1992, with the following cast:

Abenazar	Michael Bertenshaw
Rowloon	Anthony Corriette
Mrs Vizier	Chrissie Cotterill
Princess	Jackie Crawford
Emperor	Peter Durkin
Genie of the Ring	Yvonne Edgell
Aladdin	Benjamin Fellows
Sung Din	Alan Ford
Kwailing	Tracy Harper
Grand Vizier	Michael O'Connor
Inscrutable Lady	Anna Palmer
Inscrutable Lady	Karen Tomlin
Merchants	David Cauchi, Pierre Fabre, Eddie St Clair-Cummins

Directed by Philip Hedley
Assistant Director and Choreographer: Karen Rabinowitz
Designed by Jenny Tiramani
Lighting by Stephen Watson
Musical Director: Robert Pettigrew
Sound Design by Derrick Zieba
Magic Adviser: Simon Slater
Musicians: Robert Pettigrew (Synthesizer/Flute), Brian Protheroe (Piano), Brian Shields (Double Bass/Flute)
Production Manager: Bob Irwin
Stage Manager: Helen Drew
Deputy Stage Managers: Anna Hill and Angie Wallis

CHARACTERS

Male

Aladdin, adolescent
Abenazar, his wicked uncle
Rowloon, a well-bred young man
The Grand Vizier, Rowloon's father
The Emperor of China
Sung Din, Aladdin's mother
The Genie of the Lamp, a male voice

Female

Kwailing, Aladdin's adolescent friend
Mrs Vizier, Rowloon's mother
The Crown Princess of China, adolescent
The First Inscrutable Lady
The Second Inscrutable Lady
The Genie of the Ring

Merchants, Servants etc.

SYNOPSIS OF SCENES

ACT I	Scene 1	A Desert
	Scene 2	China's most ancient city
	Scene 3	The Royal Palace
	Scene 4	Outside Aladdin's house
	Scene 5	Front-cloth
	Scene 6	Aladdin's house
	Scene 7	The Royal Palace
	Scene 8	The Market
	Scene 9	Outside Aladdin's house
	Scene 10	The Journey/A Mountain
	Scene 11	Inside the Cave
ACT II	Scene 1	Inside the Cave
	Scene 2	Sung Din's house
	Scene 3	The Desert
	Scene 4	The Royal Palace
	Scene 5	The Market
	Scene 6	The Royal Palace/New Palace/Front-cloth
	Scene 7	Front-cloth/New Palace
	Scene 8	A Garden/Front-cloth
	Scene 9	Song Sheet
	Scene 10	New Palace in the Desert
	Scene 11	New Palace at Home

MUSICAL NUMBERS

ACT I

1. **I'll Make The World My Own** — Abenazar
2. **Chinese Upper Crust** — Merchants
3. **Bored** — Aladdin, Merchants
4. **Out There** — Princess
5. **An Uncle's Joy** — Abenazar and two Neighbours
6. **Out There** (Reprise) — Princess, Aladdin, Kwailing
7. **Little Shop** — Sung Din, Aladdin, Abenazar, Kwailing, Merchants
8. **Golden Boy** — Abenazar, Aladdin, Sung Din, Kwailing, Shopkeepers
9. **What A Day** — Abenazar, Kwailing, Sung Din, Aladdin

ACT II

10. **We'll Never Be Poor Again** — Aladdin, Kwailing, Sung Din
11. **I'll Love You Darling Daddy When I'm Clean** — Princess, Emperor, Inscrutable Ladies, Grand Vizier, Mrs Vizier, Rowloon
12. **I Got The Price I Asked For** — Aladdin, Merchants, Sung Din, Kwailing, Grand Vizier, Mrs Vizier, Rowloon
13. **A Girl Like This** — Aladdin, Princess
14. **He's Suitable, He's Suitable** — Grand Vizier, Mrs Vizier, Inscrutable Ladies, Emperor, Aladdin, Sung Din, Genie of the Ring
15. **With Grit And Gumption** — Sung Din
16. **When Everybody's Happy But You** — Kwailing, Rowloon
17. **Fly, Fly, Fly** — Genie of the Ring
18. **Magic** — All

The Vocal Score for this pantomime is available from Samuel French Ltd.

ACT I

Scene 1

A Desert

The wind can be heard. The Light is dim. A fire glows

Standing next to the fire is Abenazar. He throws some sand on to the fire and flames leap up

Abenazar Right then, show me! Show me I where I can get the power!

A mysterious female voice comes from off stage

Voice No!

Abenazar Yes! I've learnt the magic rituals! (*He throws more sand on to the fire, which flames again*) I've called you to my fireside so you must speak, that I may come alive truly! Speak! (*He throws more sand on to the fire*)

There is a clap of thunder

Voice In China's most ancient city, you will find a cave where lie enormous riches. Therein also lies a magic lamp that will make you greater than all the rulers of the world.

Abenazar Oh, oh, wonderful, precisely what I want!

Voice But this lamp can only be brought out by a young boy, a boy so worthless, so disliked, that no-one would ever trust him to do anything good. Now leave me!

There is more thunder and the fire flames again

Abenazar Free! At last I'm free to do everything anyone would ever want to do in all their lives!

Song 1: I'll Make The World My Own

(*Singing*) I'll get drunk,
I'll get high,

I will live on milk and honey till
The bees run dry!

I'll have dosh,
I'll have clout,
And if anyone complains they'll
Have their gums pulled out.

I will rule the world in splendour
From a golden throne of state
Where the cushions are the faces of
The people that I hate.
If they splutter, grunt or mutter
They will all be turned to stone
As I make this little world of ours my own.

I will zoom
Like a bat!
I will whisk away old ladies and
Then drop them flat.

As I soar
Through the sky
I will make the sun get hotter so
The seas go dry!

I will rove around the planets
And play snooker with them all;
I will use the stars as conkers and
Kick Earth round like a ball;
And you'll all sing you'll adore me in
A sweet harmonious tone

Chorus (*off*) Allelujah!

Abenazar As I simply make the universe,
The big and bouncing universe,
The most amusing universe,
My own, my own, my very very own!
Ha!

(*Speaking; to the audience*) Now to find a worthless boy. Oh, but in China. What a pity.

He exits

Scene 2

China's most ancient city

There is a row of shop fronts on the stage

Many gongs sound. A crowd of smiling Chinese merchants in velvet hats, with long moustaches and pigtails, issue from their shops

Song 2: Chinese Upper Crust

Merchants

Here in China's ancient city
Trading is the nitty gritty.
We work hard to swell our kitty;
We're the upper crust.

We sell lots of T'angs and Mings and
Willow pattern plates and things and
We all grow as rich as kings and
We do not go bust.

Chorus

Ping-pong
Upper crust,
Yen on yen,
No go bust,
Very charming
Upper crust,
Inscrutably disarming
Upper crust.

Ever calm and ever smiling
People find us so beguiling
That we simply go on piling
Money thick as dust.

Sensitive to every feeling,
Such good manners in our dealing
Keep us, since we're so appealing,
In the upper crust.

Repeat chorus

Aladdin (*off*) Sha - ame! You'll get shame up! Deee - stress!
Merchants Aah! Aladdin! Aladdin, horrid boy!
First Merchant Empty.
Second Merchant Idle!
Third Merchant And socially undesirable!
All Merchants Aaaaaaah!

The Merchants raise their hands all together and shuffle off as Aladdin backs on, shouting. Aladdin is fifteen and is carrying a bag of chocolates

Aladdin You big girl's blouse, you! (*He pops a chocolate in his mouth*)

Rowloon and Kwailing enter. Rowloon is nineteen but has the manner of a middle-aged man; Kwailing is fifteen

Rowloon I'm very nice, very kind, I love nature, and give me my chockies back.
Aladdin Orange creams. Mmm. (*He throws a chocolate to Kwailing*) Kwailing.
Kwailing Thanks.
Rowloon (*to Kwailing*) They're mine! They're my favourites! I get them from a nice little man on the corner, and one day I'll be Emperor.
Kwailing Give them back, Aladdin.
Aladdin (*putting a pebble in the bag of sweets and throwing the bag to Rowloon*) Here you are then.
Rowloon Thank you.
Aladdin And off you go.
Kwailing Are you the Emperor's son?
Rowloon (*eating a chocolate*) He hasn't got one. But I'm going to marry his daughter, the Crown Princess. Father says so.
Kwailing Father?
Rowloon He's the Grand Vizier, the Emperor's best friend and helper. (*To Aladdin*) What's your father?

Aladdin Dead.

Rowloon Oh, oh, I am so sorry. Have another orange cream.

Aladdin No, thanks. (*To Kwailing, indicating that she should leave with him*) Kwailing?

Rowloon Don't go. I'll have another one. (*He takes the pebble out of the bag and holds the bag out to Kwailing*) And you. And we'll all have an orange cream picnic to cheer ourselves up.

Kwailing (*taking a chocolate*) Thank you.

Aladdin (*indicating with his head that he and Kwailing should leave*) Kwailing!

Rowloon (*popping the pebble in his mouth*) That's better. I like it when things are nice. (*He bites the pebble*) Aaaah! My teeth! It's a stone!

Aladdin Time to go! (*He moves away*)

Rowloon You horrid, horrid person, you did it on purpose!

Kwailing Aladdin!

Aladdin (*turning to Kwailing*) Me?

Rowloon I bet you don't love nature at all. I hate you!

Aladdin Don't you have a go at me for giving back your rotten orange creams that probably fell off the back of a rickshaw, you great wet wimp of a father's boy!

Rowloon I got them from a nice little man ...

Abenazar and two of the Merchants enter

Song 3: Bored

Aladdin

No-one ever tries to see
The problem that's affecting me —
I'm bored!

I'm very rough and very wild,
And people call me a wicked child —
I'm bored!

They say that I'm an awful pest
And never give the world a rest,
But that's the only way I know
To get the fun I long for, so
Just don't expect a little dear
'Cos nothing's going to change in here,
I'm bored.

Chorus

Merchants He's so bored, he's really bored
Bored as bored as — ah ah, he's bored.

Aladdin I want to scream, I want to shout
And knock the other kids about —
I'm bored.

I want to do amazing tricks
And get on other people's wicks,
I want excitement to the core,
I want it more and more and more,
I want the sky, I want the sun,
I want to be the number one,
I'm bored.

The first verse is repeated

Aladdin (*speaking*) Come on, Kwailing, let's leave them.

Aladdin and Kwailing exit

Abenazar enters

Abenazar Hah. A truly worthless, no-good, idle boy, yes?
All Yes.
Abenazar Excellent. I believe I'm related to him.
Rowloon What jolly bad luck.
Abenazar And if he doesn't turn out to be worthless enough, I've got my eyes on you (*he turns to the audience*) and you, and you, and you. Oh, ha ha! The joys of evil! Now where does he live, d'you say?
First Merchant With his widowed mother, Sung Din.
Abenazar *Widowed* mother! Excellent!

Abenazar exits

Rowloon What a horrid morning. I'm going to the palace where it's all nice.

Rowloon exits

Scene 3

The Royal Palace

The Grand Vizier, Mrs Vizier and Rowloon enter

Grand Vizier Right. This is the Royal Palace, I'm the Grand Vizier and this is my wife ——

Rowloon Mummy.

Mrs Vizier And this is our son, Rowloon ——

Rowloon We've met.

Grand Vizier And we're anxious to get the Emperor to name a date for his wedding to the Crown Princess.

Mrs Vizier One does like these things settled.

A gong sounds loudly

Grand Vizier Eyes down, everyone.

Mrs Vizier What?

Grand Vizier Eyes closed. The Crown Princess is coming and no-one is allowed to see her.

Rowloon Even I haven't seen her, and I'm engaged to her.

Mrs Vizier(*to the audience*) So if you'd all just close your eyes for a teeny tiny while, and no peeping.

The gong sounds again

Grand Vizier That's it. She's coming.

Mrs Vizier And here we go.

They all close their eyes

Rowloon (*putting his hands over his eyes; excitedly*) Oooh!

The Princess enters

Princess Oh, for crying out loud, this is ridiculous. (*To the audience*) Come on, look at me, all of you.

Grand Vizier It's not allowed, Your Highness.

Princess Have a really good look, come on.

Rowloon No! Stop her being so peculiar, Father.
Grand Vizier Your Highness, I think perhaps you don't understand——

Everyone except Rowloon opens his or her eyes

Princess That's it. Good. And may I say I don't want any more eye-shutting stuff? It's really frustrating, no-one looking at you when you're the loveliest girl in the world.
Mrs Vizier These people are what we call common, Your Highness.
Rowloon (*still with his eyes shut*) I'm not common. Look, eyes shut, upper crust, can't see a thing.
Princess Yes, well, that's your problem. Why does Daddy want to speak to me?
Grand Vizier It could be about a matter of great importance that would make you less lonely.
Rowloon Our wedding day, in fact, ha ha ha ha ha.
Princess Oh no.
Rowloon (*looking*) What? Oh! Oh, you're beautiful! You're absolutely wonderful!
Princess Yes, I know. And I'd love to be able to say that to someone else.
Rowloon Since we're engaged, why not say it to me?

There are huge gong noises

Grand Vizier The Emperor! This time it is eyes shut! Eyes everyone, eyes.
Princess Oh, do stop it.
Rowloon She was just going to say that I'm absolutely wonderful.
Princess It's only Daddy. If he dares to touch them I'll run away from home.
Rowloon No! You mustn't do that!
Mrs Vizier No.
Princess Just look, everyone.
Rowloon No!
Grand Vizier I can't accept responsibility for this. If the Emperor has your heads chopped off it's not my fault, though it could be fun.

There is a big gong sound

Rowloon (*with his hands over his eyes; anxiously*) Oh, Lord!

The Emperor enters followed by his two acolytes, First Inscrutable Lady and Second Inscrutable Lady

Emperor Everyone's gazing.

First Inscrutable Lady
Second Inscrutable Lady } (*together*) Horrors! Oh horrors!

Emperor Grand Vizier, you'll have to execute them.

First Inscrutable Lady
Second Inscrutable Lady } (*together*) All of them.

Rowloon Not me, look, eyes shut, very suitable, me.

Grand Vizier Right. (*He draws his sword and advances into the audience*) I'll just start on this little lot here.

The Princess intervenes, pummelling the Grand Vizier and dragging him back to the stage

Princess No! No! Stop it, you silly man! (*To the Emperor, eventually*) Daddy, if these people get executed, I'll run away from home.

Emperor No!

Princess Yes!

Emperor (*to the audience*) She always does this to me! I love her very much, but she does make me swear! Damn!

First Inscrutable Lady
Second Inscrutable Lady } (*together, shocked*) Oh!

Mrs Vizier There, there, Your Majesty, she needs a woman's voice. Just let her have her way over this and I'll make things go nicely for you.

Emperor How?

Mrs Vizier If she were married to Rowloon, like you promised, she'd live in her own palace.

Emperor Ah, peace!

Mrs Vizier So just let her have her way in this matter and she'll do anything you ask.

Emperor Really? All right then, everyone can look at me without having their heads cut off.

Princess And me.

Emperor No.

Princess Yes. (*She gets the audience to agree*)

Emperor All right! And at you!

Rowloon Well, I'm going to be very nice and keep my eyes shut, because I know you prefer people that way.

Mrs Vizier Ah. He's so thoughtful.

Grand Vizier Good lad.

Emperor He's a creep.

Mrs Vizier So name his wedding day.

Grand Vizier As a reward for being creepish.

Princess But I can't say he's wonderful.

Mrs Vizier He's got a sweet personality.

Emperor And he's the only suitable person we know, so the wedding will take place the day after the Princess's next birthday, which is in six months' time.

Mrs Vizier Perfect.

Princess No!

Emperor Cheer up. You'll learn to love him. People do.

First Inscrutable Lady
Second Inscrutable Lady } (*together*) Hooray, hooray and long live the Emperor.

First Inscrutable Lady (*to audience*) That's the sort of thing we say.

First Inscrutable Lady
Second Inscrutable Lady } (*together*) Hooray, hooray.

Second Inscrutable Lady And jolly, jolly good.

Grand Vizier And we're deeply, cringingly grateful, Your Majesty.

Emperor Of course. The court will now retire to sit for three hours in the lotus position until lunch.

Second Inscrutable Lady Goody.

First Inscrutable Lady (*to the audience*) It's what we always do.

The Emperor heads for the exit, leading everyone except the Princess off in a procession, Mrs Vizier bringing up the rear

Emperor After that we'll receive any presents our poor and humble citizens have brought us.

Second Inscrutable Lady We always do that, too.

Emperor Doing the usual thing makes us all feel comfy.

The Emperor exits, followed by the others

Mrs Vizier (*about to leave: to the Princess*) From now on all the presents will be for you, dear, so make a wedding list. It's the usual thing.

Mrs Vizier exits, leaving the Princess alone

Song 4: Out There

Princess Butter dishes, cheese boards, toast racks
And stuff to help you cook,
Bedclothes, china and a reading lamp
And a useless visitors' book ——

The thought of it all is dreadful
For I haven't yet had my life,
And I just don't want the usual thing,
Nor to be a usual wife.

I want to
Mooch around the town,
See sights and wander slowly up and down,
Make friends and talk to people in the street,
People you can meet,
Out there, out there.

I want to
Hang about the shops,
Buy postcards and eat purple lollipops,
Go dancing when the moon is up and sing
Loud as anything,
Out there, out there.

I don't want to enter into marriage
Anchored to the palace and the throne,
When I haven't been allowed
To mingle with the crowd
Or gone to have adventures of my own.

I want to
Swim out in the sea
As dawn is breaking, have a picnic tea
In woody glades with sausages and then
Do it all again.
Out there,
Where the air is so rare,
Out there, out there.

(*Speaking*) In fact, blow the lotus position, blow getting married, I'm off.

She exits

Scene 4

Outside Aladdin's house

Sung Din, Aladdin's mother, enters with Kwailing. Sung Din is carrying several swathes of cloth and, during the following scene, she piles the swathes into Kwailing's arms until the girl disappears from view

Sung Din I don't want excuses, I want my son.
Kwailing I don't know where ——
Sung Din I want him here, working for me, and working for nothing. (*Bellowing*) Aladdin?
Kwailing I don't think he's ——
Sung Din (*to the audience*) I'm a poor widow and I don't like it, do I.
Kwailing No.
Sung Din (*to the audience*) And all day long I weave this stuff in the back parlour and send someone out to sell it and they never get more than one lousy yen for a barrowload and I'm broke and fed up and undignified. (*Calling*) Aladdin!
Kwailing This is getting rather too heavy to ——
Sung Din (*to the audience*) From the moment he was born that boy's been trouble.
Kwailing (*to the audience*) She doesn't like him.
Sung Din I'd never have married the late Mr Din if I'd known his son was going to turn out the way he has. I was used to better things once because my father was a great man, a Mandarin, wise, clever, handsome, proud ——
Kwailing So you've said.

Kwailing vanishes behind the pile of cloth

Sung Din (*to the audience*) He loved us. He whipped us twice a day and loved us. (*To Kwailing, barely pausing for breath*) Where've you gone?

Kwailing (*staggering under the weight*) I'm here.

Sung Din Well, don't hang about. Deliver this to the stupid cloth merchant and tell him if he wants me to weave another inch he'll have to go down on his knees.

Kwailing He'll just go to some other weaver, Sung Din.

Sung Din Mrs Din to you. And you tell him if he goes to another weaver he's no longer part of my set.

Aladdin enters, pushing a barrow

Ah, so you've turned up.

Aladdin Hallo, Mother.

Sung Din I've been up since five this morning, working, feeling bitter, and you've done nothing but live I suppose.

Aladdin That's right.

Sung Din You killed your father, you know, killed him by not being easy to bring up. Didn't he, my love? (*Shouting towards the earth*) Can you hear me, my poor dead husband? It's your dear wife, still wrestling with your dreadful son, who's still idle, useless, empty, a nothing — that's what you are, a nothing, (*to Kwailing*) that's what he is, love, nothing, nothing, nothing at all.

Kwailing He's lovely, Mrs Din.

Sung Din Two of you, now, is it? Well, get off with all that cloth I've woven and tell those absurd men in the market they won't get any better cloth anywhere than that.

Abenazar enters

(Without so much as drawing breath) And who the bleeding hell are you?

Abenazar A visitor from a distant land.

Sung Din We don't want any of those, so clear off.

Abenazar Dear lady, overworked, bringing up a family, I do understand.

Sung Din No-one understands! I'm going home to dream great things, which is all I can do, because I'm skint, skint, skint, skint. Got it?

Abenazar Aah.

Sung Din And you two get moving while I go off and remember.

Sung Din exits

Aladdin (*upsetting all the cloth and stamping on it*) Stupid woman, stupid cloth, work, work, work, never any joy — I hate it all.

Kwailing Stop it, Aladdin. She's been weaving for days to make that.

Abenazar Oh dear, oh dear, oh dear. Who's an upset laddie then?

Aladdin Me. So what?

Abenazar Perhaps underneath your anger you are dear, sweet and charming.

Kwailing No, he isn't. He's just nice.

Aladdin (*to Abenazar*) Who *are* you?

Abenazar (*to the audience*) Now, watch this. (*To Aladdin*). My boy, my dear boy, are you not Aladdin, the son of Mr Din, the famous tailor of this city?

Aladdin My dad's been dead for ages.

Abenazar (*in great perturbation*) Ah! Oh! Oh! Ah! (*He bursts into tears*) Oh my poor lad! My poor dear little fellow. (*He embraces Aladdin*)

Aladdin Hey!

Kwailing Watch it.

Abenazar (*crying even more*) Poor lost child!

Aladdin Lay off, will you.

Kwailing What's it all about, Mister?

Abenazar I'm sorry. The news upset me. How can I help weeping when I hear of my own brother's death?

Aladdin Brother?

Abenazar I have been travelling the world for many years and returned home in the hope of once again seeing poor — er — er —

Aladdin Hassan.

Abenazar Hassan, my own beloved brother and now you tell me he's ... (*He gulps*) When I left here, he wasn't even married, and now he's ... (*He gulps*)

Aladdin Goodness.

Kwailing Heavens.

Abenazar But the moment I saw you I knew you must be his boy. Your grace, your elegance — welcome, nephew!

Aladdin You're my uncle? Really?

Abenazar Let me be more than Uncle. Let me take Hassan's place and be ——

Aladdin You've seen my mother.

Abenazar Poor lady. Wracked by poverty. (*He hands Aladdin some gold coins*) Here.

Aladdin Crikey.

Kwailing Wow.

Abenazar Oh, but money is nothing compared with the ties of blood. Neighbours, friends, come and bear witness to the power of the family and the meaning of an uncle's affection.

Neighbours enter

First Neighbour It clearly means a very great deal.

Second Neighbour About five hundred yen by the look of it.

Song 5: An Uncle's Joy

Abenazar

There's a sad sad heart here sighing
For the family I held so dear,
And an ancient eye that's crying
With a lonesome and lovelorn tear.
Through years I've toiled and I've roughed it
With a dream that has fed my soul
Of a brother who seems to have snuffed it
And his son who is on the dole.

Chorus

So come to my arms to be nurtured
You deprived and fatherless boy,
Be firm, grow strong, drink deep and very long
From the wells of an uncle's joy.

Though chance has stopped me sharing
In the growth of this sapling brave,
I now pledge him all my caring
Till I go to my stone cold grave.
The night of his grief it is over
And he needs no more to be sad,
For I'll see that he lives in clover
When he treats me as dear old Dad.

Repeat chorus

For I will give you the laughter
And the love that is due to a son,
And I'll go to the great hereafter
With the sense of a deed well done.

Repeat chorus

Aladdin Uncle!
Abenazar Uncle Abenazar.
Neighbours His real uncle!
Kwailing So he says, anyway.
Abenazar And tonight I'll dine at your house. Buy the food and I will bring presents for your mother.
Aladdin I'm sure she'll be glad to see you. (*He calls off*) Mother!
Abenazar No, no. Let it all come as a beautiful surprise.
First Neighbour It'll do that all right. I never knew Hassan had a brother.
Second Neighbour Isn't it all charming?
Abenazar But of course. That's what I am. Till tonight, then. (*To the audience*) What a little fool, so different from me.

He exits

Aladdin Come on, Kwai.
Kwailing He's very kind, but I don't really trust him.
Aladdin I do. I'm a deprived and fatherless boy. It's great!

They exit

Scene 5

A front-cloth is dropped in

The Princess walks through the auditorium, wearing clothes that indicate she has been "out there"

Princess Done it. And it's a bit scary. I mean — all those people, with their eyes open. I must be bold, though. Come on, Princess, show your mettle. (*She gets up on to the stage*)

Kwailing and Aladdin enter

Hallo there, hahaha.
Kwailing Funny voice.
Aladdin Are you the sort that buys chocolates from a nice little man outside the palace?

Princess What?
Aladdin Forget it.
Kwailing Bye.
Princess Are you doing anything special just now?
Kwailing We're going shopping if you must know.
Princess Can I come, too?
Kwailing No.
Aladdin Yes.
Kwailing No, Aladdin.
Aladdin Yes! You're so off everyone today, Kwai.
Kwailing We've got so much to do, buying food, and there'll be more cloth to deliver ——
Aladdin We'll manage it, all right? Just keep cool.
Princess I only want to come along with you, that's all. Please?
Kwailing Come along with us.[2]

Song 6: Out There (Reprise)

Princess
I want to
Mooch around the town,
See sights and wander slowly up and down.

Princess
Aladdin }
Make friends and talk to people in the street
People you can meet
Out here, out here.

We want to
Hang about the shops,
Buy postcards and eat purple lollipops.

The Princess and Aladdin persuade Kwailing to join in

Princess
Aladdin }
Kwailing
Go dancing when the moon is up and sing
Loud as anything
Out here, out here.

We don't want to hassle or to worry,
Thinking of the things we have to do,
For the sun is riding high,
And summer's drifting by

And no-one seems to matter, only—
(*They look from one to another along the line*)
You — you — you ——

So let us
Swim out in the sea
As dawn is breaking, have a picnic tea
In woody glades with sausages, and then,
Do it all again.
Out here,
Where the air is so clear,
Out here, out here.

Mrs Vizier and the Grand Vizier enter

Mrs Vizier Ah! My dear! Your father's been so worried about you.

Grand Vizier He thinks he may have to go back on his word about certain things.

Aladdin What's the matter?

Princess Sorry. I've got to go.

Grand Vizier (*drawing his sword*) Oh no!

Princess Oh!

Kwailing Stop it!

Aladdin (*to the Princess, indicating the audience*) Quick. Down there.

Princess Thank you. (*She runs into the audience*)

Mrs Vizier No! Among the vulgar! Stop her! (*She runs into the audience*)

Grand Vizier (*running into the audience brandishing his sword*) Stop her! Stop her!

Aladdin Crikey! (*He points in the wrong direction*) She's over there! (*In another direction*) She's over there!

The Princess escapes back on to the stage

Princess Thanks.

Aladdin Quick, this way.

The Princess heads for the exit

Rowloon (*off*) Have you found her? Father, Mummy?

Grand Vizier Nearly!

Princess Rowloon, the Emperor's coming! Shut your eyes.(*To Aladdin and Kwailing)* We'll meet again.
Aladdin I hope so.

The Princess runs off in the opposite direction to Rowloon

Rowloon *(off)* Mummy?
Aladdin It's that prune with the orange cream chocs. Let's go.
Kwailing Funny voices, funny people.

Aladdin and Kwailing exit

Grand Vizier (*returning to the stage*) She's gone.
Mrs Vizier (*returning to the stage*) Escaped.

Rowloon enters with his eyes shut

Rowloon Where's the Emperor?
Grand Vizier Open your silly eyes. There is no Emperor.
Rowloon Oh. (*He opens his eyes*) Then where's She Whom I Adore?
Grand Vizier I don't know, but I'm beginning to think she's too clever for you. Keep looking.

They all head for the exit

Rowloon Women aren't clever. They're cosy.
Mrs Vizier I never taught you that, my son.

They all exit

Scene 6

Aladdin's house

Sung Din stands with a glass of sherry in her hand

Sung Din You see? Decayed gentlewoman. This is all I have left from the gracious life; one little glass of dry sherry before the evening crust to remind me I was once someone. Thank heavens, my father, the Mandarin, never lived to see this.

Aladdin and Kwailing enter with loads of food, including several purple lollipops

Aladdin Mother? Get your false teeth in, we're going to have a real chomp tonight.
Sung Din You've been stealing again.
Kwailing He hasn't.
Aladdin It's a present.
Sung Din Or worse, you spent all my hard-earned money on it.
Kwailing He didn't.
Aladdin Look, my uncle gave me money to buy food so you could make a wonderful meal and he's coming tonight to eat it so stop picking on me and get cooking.
Sung Din You haven't got an uncle. Your father was an only son, and spoilt, like you all are.
Aladdin I have an uncle, he's wonderful, it's a miracle, and if you're too stupid to see it then I'm ——
Sung Din What d'you mean, a miracle?

There is a knock at the door

Aladdin Open that and see.

Sung Din opens the door

A Servant enters with a large basket of fruits and wines

Kwailing Oh! It is pretty!
Sung Din It's a miracle! It is a miracle! And very well deserved, too. We used to have all that before my marriage, when my father was alive. The fruits and wines ——

Abenazar appears

Abenazar Does my gift please you, most gracious lady?
Sung Din Did you do this?
Abenazar To please you.
Sung Din I told you to hop it. (*To the audience*) Nothing but trouble, his sort.
Abenazar Dearest madam, sweet little Hassan, your husband, was my

brother, and I am deeply, truly, quite quite shatteringly heartbroken to hear of his death.

Sung Din Oh?

Abenazar So I've brought these little gifts to cheer us all up in some small way.

Sung Din You hear that? He's your father's rich brother —— *rich* brother?

Abenazar Yes. Is this enough for the evening?

Sung Din For the evening? Oh, yes, for the evening, just for the evening.

Abenazar (*to the Servant*) You can go then.

Sung Din (*opening a bottle of wine*) There is a likeness to my husband, now I look at you. Don't you think so, Aladdin?

Kwailing Not really.

Aladdin He's much nicer than anyone I've ever known.

Abenazar Dear boy. And did you follow your father's trade and become a tailor?

Sung Din Did he heck. My son, Mr — er — er —

Abenazar Abenazar.

Sung Din Abenazar — rather mystic, that, charming in its way, of course — well, my son, Mr Abenazar ——

Aladdin — is bored out of his tiny mind with people always saying he has to settle down, yeah, how he has to become a boring tailor, yeah. I don't want any of that, no, I don't.

Kwailing Aladdin!

Sung Din (*talking towards the earth*) You hear that, you stupid tailor? That's your son, failing to support his mother, that's your boy, a chip off your old block not mine, your miserable family (*to Abenazar*) — no insult intended, of course, the food's lovely, and the wine — (*to the earth again*) but money doesn't grow on trees, and you never got that through your son's thick head, did you, you clapped out old clothier.

Abenazar Money could come from a shop. Would you like a shop, Aladdin? And smart clothes? Become a merchant? A big name around the town? Right on?

Aladdin Yes, I'd like that. I'd like to go strutting about in a shop.

Abenazar I'll buy you one, then.

Kwailing You won't.

Abenazar I will.

Kwailing You won't.

Abenazar I will, I will, I will! I promise!

Kwailing Really?

Abenazar Yes. So stop being suspicious.
Aladdin Yes.
Sung Din And rude.
Kwailing All right!
Sung Din And welcome, my husband's brother, whom I never doubted for a minute. The most brilliant, brilliant, brilliant organizer of family finances I've ever met.
Aladdin I told you, Mother, he's wonderful.

Song 7: Little Shop

Sung Din
Aladdin }

We'll have a little shop
Where the till goes ping
And each little ring
Brings butter and jam
And eggs and ham
And sugar and tea
And we will see
What fun it is to have a little shop.

Abenazar

We'll have a little shop
That is rather large,
Not butter and marge
But silver and gold
And things untold,
Like priceless gems
From which there stems
A future that is lots of little shops.

All

We'll have a little shop
It will be tip-top
And we'll see
What fun it will be
To have a shop.

We'll have our little shops
All over the place
And our boy's face
Will be famous far
And wide and our
Good fortune will

Continue till
There are millions
And billions
And trillions
And zillions
Of our own,
Very own,
Little shops,
Where the till goes ping
And each little ring

Aladdin
Kwailing } Brings butter and jam
And eggs and ham

Abenazar And silver and gold
And things untold

Aladdin
Kwailing
Sung Din } And sugar and tea
And we will see

All What fun it is to have a little shop.

The Merchants appear in the shop windows

Merchants They'll have a little shop
It will be tip-top,
And we'll see
What fun it will be
To have a shop.

Sung Din (*speaking*) That's it! We're made! Get the food moving, Aladdin, and think how proud my father, the Mandarin would've been if he'd known. (*Calling down to the earth*) And you, you worm-eaten relic, thank goodness you had a decent brother, at any rate.

Abenazar Just simple-hearted and kind. Let us share our good fortune with others, shall we? You see, I'm frightfully nice, really. (*He starts to throw purple lollipops from the pile of food into the audience*)

There is a reprise of the last part of "Little Shop"

Scene 7

The Royal Palace

The Emperor is repeatedly hitting a cushion held by one of the Inscrutable Ladies. The Ladies are striking little bells in time to his blows

Emperor I'm angry, I'm angry, I'm angry, I'm angry, I'm angry.
First Inscrutable Lady Better?
Emperor No.
Second Inscrutable Lady Try some more.
Emperor (*attacking the cushion again*) Even though I let everyone look at me, she went away, leaving me, who is her be-all and end-all, the only person who understands her, the light of her life, protector and adviser and everything wonderful!
First Inscrutable Lady Better now?
Emperor Not much. The fact is she broke her promise and that is unforgivable.
First Inscrutable Lady }
Second Inscrutable Lady } (*together*) Chop her head off.
Second Inscrutable Lady How exciting!
First Inscrutable Lady What fun!
Emperor Yes. No! We'll just go back to the old rules of no-one looking at her. Ah!

The Princess enters, her hands tied, with the Grand Vizier behind her, pushing her with his sword. Rowloon and Mrs Vizier are with them

Emperor You've found her.
Rowloon Thank heavens. Don't be too rough with that sword, I'm going to marry her.
Emperor Where've you been? Don't tell me! I'm deeply angry and terribly hurt.
First Inscrutable Lady }
Second Inscrutable Lady } (*together*) Have another hit.

The Emperor hits the cushion

Princess Oh shut up.
Emperor Who?
Princess Them.
Mrs Vizier Nice little girls don't say that sort of thing, do they?

First Inscrutable Lady
Second Inscrutable Lady } (*together*) No.
Mrs Vizier They behave, don't they?
First Inscrutable Lady
Second Inscrutable Lady } (*together*) Yes.
Grand Vizier Exactly, Hilda.
Emperor Hilda?
Mrs Vizier Me.
Emperor Oh! Well, what've you got to say?
Princess I've enjoyed myself.
First Inscrutable Lady
Second Inscrutable Lady } (*together; shocked*) Horrors!
Emperor How?
Princess Doing things.
Grand Vizier What things?
Emperor Dangerous things?
Grand Vizier Wicked things?
Rowloon Clever things?
Mrs Vizier Magic things?
All Oh! Horrors!
First Inscrutable Lady
Second Inscrutable Lady } (*together*) Magic is against the law.
Emperor It upsets everything.
Princess I met people.
Emperor That's just as bad! (*He starts hitting the cushion again*) I knew there was a good reason for people keeping their eyes shut. Once everyone goes around with them open, there's no knowing who they'll meet. Take her away, Grand Vizier, and you, too, Hilda. (*To the audience*) How did that happen?(*To the Grand Vizier and Mrs Vizier*) Take her to a dungeon and keep her locked up till her wedding day.
Rowloon You can't do that.
Princess No, you can't.
Emperor Oh, yes I can.
Princess Oh, no you can't.

The audience are encouraged to join in with the usual "Oh, yes I can","Oh no you can't" business

Emperor Stop them! Stop them! It's revolution!
Princess No dungeon?

Emperor All right. No dungeon. But guard her closely while I go off to the lotus position to have a little cry. Hilda, what a stupid name.
Princess I'll think of a way to get out there again. Oh! Don't you go to the public baths occasionally?
Mrs Vizier That's none of your business.
Princess It might be, you never know. Do I talk funny?
Mrs Vizier Of course not; everyone else does.

Everyone exits

Scene 8

The Market

It is evening and the shops are all lit with flares. Shopkeepers stand in their shop doorways

Abenazar, Aladdin, Sung Din and Kwailing enter

Abenazar And here we are, shops and shops and shops and shops. Take your pick.
Aladdin It's hard to say. What do you think, Kwai?
Sung Din Can't we have them all?
Abenazar Not to begin with.
Sung Din Tomorrow, then.
Abenazar Patience, Mrs Din, patience.
Sung Din That's for other people. The really interesting don't have any.
Aladdin A sweet shop, a toy shop, a knife shop ——
Kwailing A gold shop, look.
Sung Din And a jeweller's, get a jeweller's, then you could get me some enviable knick-knacks to make the ladies of my circle go green.
Abenazar In time.
Sung Din Gold gnomes, solid silver ducks, and mother of pearl everywhere.
Abenazar Alabaster picture frames, and statues of my father the Mandarin with his loving whip ——
Abenazar Silence!
Sung Din All right, all right. It costs nothing to be polite. (*Placatingly*) Nice man. (*She strokes Abenazar's arm*)

Kwailing He's rather frightening.
Aladdin Mother has that effect on people, and he's going to buy us a shop.
Kwailing Apparently.
Aladdin And I think I should have a clothes shop, because I can't become a successful merchant dressed like this.
Abenazar So true. Clothes maketh the man.
Aladdin So how does a merchant dress?
Sung Din (*looking in the shop windows*) And a merchant's mother?
Abenazar A merchant's mother waits.
Sung Din Provided she knows she's going to get a tea gown. Try this, Aladdin.

Sung Din, Abenazar and Kwailing collect a splendid, long Chinese tunic, matching trousers and a Chinese skull cap from one of the shops, and, during the following dialogue, they pull the clothes on to Aladdin

Kwailing Oh, that's lovely, put it on.
Aladdin Isn't it a dressing-gown?
Abenazar It's a sign of rank, and it's lovely.
Sung Din (*to a Shopkeeper*) My friend's paying.
Abenazar And here is the little cap of wisdom, that marks you out as a truly wise.
Kwailing You look smashing.
Aladdin Really?
Kwailing Really smashing.
Abenazar And when you've thought more deeply about it you can choose your shop tomorrow.
Aladdin Right.
Kwailing Tomorrow?
Abenazar In the meantime just enjoy being truly gorgeous. Look, everyone, at Aladdin the merchant, who is bound to succeed, (*to Kwailing*) isn't he, little lady? (*He throws some money into the shop*)

Song 8: This Golden Boy

(*Singing*) Look how his clothes
Match the gleaming in his eyes.
See how the skull cap
Proclaims that he is wise.
Note how the shoulders
Are tailored to a tee —

Tomorrow, this golden boy
Will be as rich as me.

All Rings on his fingers
And bells upon his toes;
He shall have credit
From the bank where e'er he goes.

Abenazar See how he stands
With a profile clean and high —
Tomorrow, this likely lad
Will be as rich as I.

Women Personal rickshaws
Men At sea a private junk
Abenazar Nicely equipped
Should he need to do a bunk
All Dressed like an emperor
All young and strong and slim —
Tomorrow, this wunderkind
Will be as rich as him!
Abenazar Tomorrow this golden boy
Will be as rich as me!

Sung Din Beat that, Hassan the helpless. We're on our way, and that's the first person singular.

Kwailing Oh! The shops all have a holiday tomorrow. You can't buy one.

Abenazar Oh dear, what a pity.

Aladdin The day after, then.

Abenazar Of course.

Kwailing Right, then, tomorrow I'll come round for you.

Aladdin If I'm not out with Uncle.

Abenazar We might just go for a walk, to have Men's Talk, you know, about Life, and Honour and things.

Kwailing I knew it. Something's wrong.

Aladdin Of course it isn't.

Abenazar I only need to advise him about shops. Now go home and get some sleep.

Sung Din (*smacking Kwailing's legs*) He's a lovely uncle who's bought lots of clothes so come along and don't be such a gloomy little pest.

Aladdin, stay with your uncle as long as you want, and remember I'd like a tea gown, and then (*mouthing*) lots of enviable knick-knacks.

Sung Din moves away, taking Kwailing with her

Kwailing I don't trust him!

Sung Din and Kwailing exit

Abenazar You must go home, too, boy, because tomorrow I'm going to show you wonders even greater than these clothes. I will show you jewels the size of pomegranates, caves lit by wondrous light, and power so great that the sky will tremble at it.
Aladdin Wow. Good-night, then, Uncle. You're great.
Abenazar Yes, I am. Good-night. Oh, very good-night.

Aladdin exits

The Lights in the shops go out; the market is now lit by moonlight. Abenazar chortles, then laughs louder and louder

(*Singing*) Tomorrow this golden boy
Will be as rich as me!

Scene 9

Outside Aladdin's house

Sunrise and sounds of early morning

Aladdin enters. He is in his working clothes and a headscarf and has evidently just woken up. Sung Din and Kwailing follow him, also in the process of waking up

Aladdin I haven't slept all night. I'm going to see wonders, Uncle says.
Sung Din He has a very proper sense of values, and my instincts are always right. Just do whatever he tells you.
Kwailing Something's wrong.
Aladdin It's not, Kwai. Life's going to be really good. Money, clothes,

money? I'll be back tonight, and tell you everything.

Abenazar enters with sweets

Abenazar And are we all ready for a walk into the deep countryside?
Aladdin Yeah.
Kwailing You've never gone walking in the countryside in all your life. Something is wrong, Mrs Din, I know it.
Sung Din No it's not, and my instincts are never ——
Kwailing Something is wrong.
Abenazar Oh, no it's not.
Kwailing Oh yes it is.

The audience is encouraged to join in with the usual "Oh, no it's not", "Oh yes it is" business, Sung Din leading the shouting on Abenazar's behalf. Abenazar quells the noise by throwing a lot more sweets at the audience while he says the following

Abenazar Now, now, now, now, now, now. That's better. Nothing, I promise you is going to go wrong. Really. (*Quieter*) So shut up! (*He picks out two people in the audience*) Especially you two.
Sung Din (*to the audience*) That's you lot settled.
Abenazar Dearest boy, I am now your father, and you are a young man starting out with me on the greatest journey of life. Let us go hand in hand, and travel where you have never been, hmm? (*He takes Aladdin's hand*)
Kwailing Ha.
Abenazar (*aside to Kwailing, with a big smile*) Watch it. (*To the audience*) And you.

Song 9: What A Day

(*Singing*) It's a very fine day
When the sky's all blue
And the world's all bright
And things feel new,
When every little cliché
Might come true ——

Oho! What a day!
What a day to turn into a man.

Kwailing It's cold and sharp
And bleak and grey
And it isn't at all
My kind of day
When the person I like
Is going away.
Oh dear! What a day!
What a day to lose a little friend.

Chorus

Sung Din
Aladdin } What a day, what a day today ...
Abenazar It's a very fine day
When the sky's all blue.
Kwailing It's cold and sharp
And bleak and grey.
All What a day, what a day today.

Sung Din It's a helluva day
That is tinged with gold
When you'll shift your bum
Without being told.
All (*except Sung Din)* What a day, what a day today.
Sung Din To help your mother grow
Gracefully old.
Oho! What a day!
What a day to do a bit of good.

Abenazar It's a very fine day
When the sky's all blue.
Kwailing It's cold and sharp
And bleak and grey.
Sung Din It's a helluva day
That is tinged with gold.
Aladdin It's a dangerous day
That is calling me.

The song continues through the scene change into Scene 10

Scene 10

Throughout the following journey, the sun crosses the sky and gives way to the moon

Abenazar and Aladdin walk hand in hand, leaving the others behind. They pass through the town, then farms and animals, then woodlands, then, finally, singing alone, they come to a bleak mountainous spot where a thin wind is blowing. There is a pile of stones and rocks near them; twigs are scattered about

Aladdin finishes singing his verse with slightly less confidence than before

Abenazar (*to the audience*) This is it. Oh! Oh! The perfect moment! Ooh! One more little effort and I'm there — oh!
Aladdin Uncle? This is a pretty cold place and it's getting very late.
Abenazar Ah, yes, well, I am about to show you the most beautiful garden in the world, Aladdin.
Aladdin At night?
Abenazar At night. I have travelled though centuries to reach this spot.
Aladdin Through centuries?
Abenazar Through centuries.
Aladdin But ——
Abenazar Don't question me! Just put those twigs there on those stones so we can light a fire and keep warm. Come on, come on. Do it.

Aladdin puts the twigs on the stones and Abenazar produces some matches

I'll light it, I'll light it, so stand aside. (*He lights the twigs*) Now, watch this and be astonished. (*He throws some magic powder on to the fire*)

Dense, coloured smoke and sputtering sparks come from the twigs and we hear a rumbling sound, growing louder and louder. The stones begin to fall from the pile and we have the impression that the whole earth is shaking

Earthquake music

Aladdin Uncle, it's an earthquake.
Abenazar No, no, just wait.

The rumbling continues. More stones fall from the pile

Aladdin I'm frightened. I want to get away. (*He moves away*)
Abenazar (*grabbing Aladdin*) Come back.
Aladdin (*wriggling free*) No.
Abenazar I need you.
Aladdin We'll be killed.
Abenazar You damn well stay here!

Abenazar fiercely hits Aladdin on the head; Aladdin falls to the ground

Little idiot! Just at the moment I need him! Look!

The rumbling stops as the last stones fall away to reveal a glowing marble door with a ring set into it

Abenazar (*gently smacking Aladdin's cheeks*) Wake up. Come on, wake up, laddie.

Aladdin wakes and scrambles away from Abenazar

Aladdin What did I do to deserve that?
Abenazar I hit you to start making a man of you. In truth you're dearer to me than a son, and I want to make you so rich you will almost die with the pleasure of it. (*He kisses Aladdin*)

Aladdin clasps Abenazar

(*Indicating the marble door*) Now, look there. Behind that stone is a cave only you may enter. Pull on the ring, and as you do, recite your name, your father's name, and your mother's name.

Aladdin moves to the door and takes hold of the ring. He cannot pull the door open

Aladdin Aladdin, Hassan Din, Sung Din.

The door swings open and light beams out from the cave that has been revealed

Oh!

Abenazar Now, enter.
Aladdin Me?
Abenazar Yes, you're nearly a man, I hit you, so come on, man, get in there. You will pass down into a garden with beautiful fruit growing on the trees. Don't touch them, but walk on, reciting the names like you did just now, to stop yourself turning into a stone.Then, on one of the trees, you will see a lamp, a simple lamp. Bring the lamp back to me. If you want to, you can pick the fruit at that moment.

Abenazar pushes Aladdin towards the cave

Go on.
Aladdin (*resisting*) Is it going to be very dangerous, Uncle?
Abenazar (*impatiently taking the ring from his finger*) Oh—this ring will deliver you from all dangers, so long as you do exactly as I said. Now, in.
Aladdin I'm frightened.
Abenazar You're a man, a real man! Do it for me.
Aladdin For you, Uncle.

Aladdin exits into the cave

Abenazar (*giggling suddenly*) If you can keep your head while all about you —— hahaha! I've done it! Power! (*He calls into the cave*) Keep going, my son!

The wind rises and, during the scene change, we hear Abenazar's voice echoing and re-echoing "Keep going!"

Scene 11

Inside the Cave

Here there is a garden of glittering jewel trees. The fruits on the trees look real but are, in fact, jewels. On a little terrace a tree stands with a lamp on one of its branches

Aladdin is discovered advancing through the trees, muttering his family's names over and over again

Aladdin Aladdin, Hassan Din, Sung Din (*etc. He reaches the lamp tree and sees the lamp*) This must be it.

Aladdin reaches for the lamp; as he touches it there is a little trill of quivering music. Aladdin takes the lamp and the music reaches a climax, then stops

There. Now I can go back and pick some fruit. Blimey, I wish Kwailing could see all this stuff. She'll never believe it. (*He stuffs the lamp deep into his pocket so as to free his hands and begins to gather up fruit into his arms*)

Music

Abenazar appears at the cave mouth

Abenazar Hurry! Hurry! Come on, I want the lamp.
Aladdin Coming, Uncle. (*He heads for the cave mouth*)
Abenazar Give it me.
Aladdin I've got these jewels in my arms.
Abenazar Never mind those, give it me!
Aladdin (*struggling to get the lamp free with his arms full*) I'll be with you in a minute.
Abenazar (*his anger growing out of control*) Give — it — me!
Aladdin Uncle, my arms are full ——
Abenazar GIVE — IT — ME!
Aladdin I can't reach it. Just wait.
Abenazar I can't wait! You swine, you're cheating me!
Aladdin I'm not.
Abenazar I knew you were no good from the start! They all said so and I knew it.
Aladdin You didn't!
Abenazar I did, I did! Close, cave, on this selfish, no-good youth and lock him in forever!

There is thunder. The door to the cave closes. Aladdin drops the jewels and beats on the door

Aladdin No! No! Uncle, how could you? (*He sobs and falls down in a heap*)

The CURTAIN *falls*

Kwailing enters in front of the curtain

Kwailing Aladdin? Suppertime! (*To the audience*) He's late. Perhaps we'd all better have an ice cream.

End of Act I

ACT II

Scene 1

In the Magic Cave

Aladdin is alone, sitting down and staring in front of him gloomily.The jewelledfruit, wrapped in Aladdin's headscarf, lie at hisfeet. Aladdin gets up angrily and kicks a stone

Aladdin I am not a cheat, I am not no good. But, oh, I am going to die. *(He is nearly in tears)* Well, I'm not going to die crying, I'm not. (*He puts his hands to his eyes to wipe away the tears and hurts himself with the magic ring on his finger*) Ouch, his ring.

Magic music plays

He said "It will deliver you from all dangers." (*He addresses the ring*) Ring? Take me back home and make me safe. Ring? (*He touches the ring with his other hand, then rubs the ring*)

Bigger music plays; at its climax:

The Genie of the Ring, a pretty, slightly harassed-looking lady, enters

Genie of the Ring Yes, what is it?
Aladdin Who are you?
Genie of the Ring Genie of the Ring, love. In trouble, are you?
Aladdin Yes.
Genie of the Ring Aaah. How old are you, as a matter of interest?
Aladdin Nearly sixteen.
Genie of the Ring (*appreciatively*) Oh! Big for your age. Like a sausage?

The Genie of the Ring makes a sausage appear from nowhere, as she does other items throughout the scene

Aladdin Oh.
Genie of the Ring And what's your name, if you don't mind me asking?
Aladdin Aladdin.
Genie of the Ring Mine's Gwen, Gwen of the Ring, and for the moment

I'm all yours. Come here a lot, do you? (*She causes a bottle of pop to appear*)

Aladdin I've been shut in by a man who calls himself my uncle.

Genie of the Ring I'm always having trouble with uncles. A wizard in disguise, very likely, all talk and then off in a puff of smoke. Abenazar, was it?

Aladdin Yes.

Genie of the Ring I've been all his for ages. Very nasty. I'm glad it's you now.

Aladdin Just get me out of here, then. Get me out of here.

Genie of the Ring I can't. That sort of magic's too big for me. Like to share a foo yong? (*She whisks one up by magic*)

Aladdin No.

Genie of the Ring Right. (*She makes the foo yong disappear*)

Aladdin What sort of a genie are you?

Genie of the Ring Minor, but I can keep you happy for years with tricks and things. (*She produces in succession three rabbits, a bird cage with a bird in it and a row of sparklers*) There. Call me Gwen.

Aladdin (*desperately*) I don't want to be here. I want to be home.

Genie of the Ring You want it all, you men. All right then. I don't suppose you know anything about the lamp that used to be up there.

Aladdin Yes! My uncle made me get it for him. It's here, somewhere.

Genie of the Ring Always want more than they ought, uncles. Now. (*She starts to clear things away*) Clear the decks and get that lamp ready. I know my place; always the bridesmaid and never the bride, Genie of the Ring, chief assistant to the lamp and never my own girl. Just give it a little rub and we'll see what's what.

Aladdin rubs the lamp. The Lights fade

Swelling magical music plays and there are rumbles of thunder. Mist pours down from above

Two huge lips appear. They move in time to the deep, slow speech of the Genie of the Lamp

Genie of the Lamp I am the Genie of the Lamp.

There is a roll of thunder

Who summons me?

Genie of the Ring This nice young boy Aladdin, oh Master.
Genie of the Lamp Speak your wish, Aladdin, and I will grant it.
Aladdin Genie of the Lamp, take me home to my mother and my friends. At once please. Quickly.
Genie of the Lamp To hear is to obey.

There is more thunder and more magic music. The lips fade away

Genie of the Ring (*calling*) Goodbye for now, Aladdin. I'm always here when you need me.

There are enormous wind sounds

Scene 2

Sung Din's house

Aladdin is lying on the floor, the lamp and magic fruit beside him. Sung Din is talking to the audience, oblivious to Aladdin's presence behind her

Sung Din And I shall have flock wallpaper, red and gold, a mother-of-pearl washbasin, one or two sizeable furnishings in fumed oak and a large marble fireplace in front of which to entertain the envious, of which I hope there will be many. What a rouched future I see for myself! If only I weren't so bleedin' hungry! I wonder what's keeping —— (*She sees Aladdin*) Oh! Where did you come from? Get up and tell your uncle we need food.
Aladdin Mother?
Sung Din Who else?
Aladdin I don't want to see my uncle ever again. He tried to kill me.
Sung Din What did you do to annoy him?
Aladdin Nothing. He used me to try to get his hands on some treasure and then left me to die in a deep dark cave.
Sung Din You mean there's going to be no little shops, no fortune...
Aladdin Nothing.
Sung Din I knew it! The moment I saw him I knew he was crooked. His eyes.
Aladdin He fooled you.
Sung Din And look at you, all messy, completely taken in by him. Go and wash. (*Referring to the lamp*) What's that?

Aladdin Don't touch. It's precious.
Sung Din (*taking the lamp*) We'll sell it, then, and have supper.
Aladdin No!
Sung Din I'll just go off to the kitchen to give it a polish and then you can sell it at the antique mart.

Sung Din exits

Aladdin No, mother, don't.
Sung Din (*off*) It's still open down there, so you can just pop out and——

There is a sudden clap of thunder. Sung Din screams from off stage

Aladdin (*angrily*) She never listens!

The thunder rolls on and the magic music plays loudly. Masses of mist pour from the kitchen and the voice of the Genie of the Lamp can be heard

Genie of the Lamp What is your wish?

Sung Din enters in a great hurry

Sung Din Aladdin! There's a bleeding great pair of lips floating around in the kitchen! The place is over-run with unreliable aliens!

The Genie of the Ring enters from the kitchen, coughing a little

Genie of the Ring Hallo, love, it's me.
Aladdin Oh, great.
Genie of the Ring (*to the audience*) I do the two jobs, you see, Genie of the Ring and assistant to the big fellow.
Sung Din (*to Aladdin, referring to the Genie of the Ring*) What's that?
Aladdin She's Gwen of the Ring, and she's a load of laughs.
Sung Din (*to Aladdin*) What did you do with that uncle?
Aladdin Magic. She's magic and the lamp's magic.
Sung Din And magic's against the law.
Genie of the Ring But fun! Like a popadam? (*She magically produces a popadam*)
Sung Din (*seizing the popadam*) Crumbs everywhere!
Genie of the Lamp (*off; cross*) Speak your wish!

Genie of the Ring You'd better hurry 'cause he gets impatient.
Sung Din (*calling*) Right then. If you want to know I'd like a good five course meal on a lot of silver salvers.
Genie of the Lamp To hear is to obey.

During the following speech a sumptuous meal, served on silver salvers, appears, ushered in by the Genie of the Ring

Sung Din I should think so, too, your sort. And then clear off back where you came from, both of you, and stop teaching my boy things he's too young to understand. (*She sees the meal*) Good heavens!
Aladdin Wow!
Genie of the Ring He understands, don't you, love? And people often say thank you.
Aladdin Thank *you*!
Sung Din Very nice. We're much obliged.
Genie of the Ring Anything else before I go?
Sung Din (*dipping a finger into one of the dishes and tasting it*) Salt.

Salt magically appears

Oh! (*To the Genie of the Ring*) You're obviously trying to be a pleasant person. Well done.
Genie of the Ring It's not too difficult if you try. Toodleoo.

There is a flash, under cover of which:

The Genie of the Ring exits

Sung Din Beware of women who move fast, they don't stop.

Kwailing bursts in

Kwailing Mrs Din, I have to know —— (*She sees Aladdin*) Oh, you're back! (*She rushes up to Aladdin and hugs him*)
Sung Din The place is full of pert girls. Put him down!
Kwailing (*to Aladdin*) Are you all right?
Aladdin (*referring to the feast*) Just look.
Kwailing (*gazing at the feast*) Wow.
Sung Din Of course, his uncle tried to kill him like I knew he would ——

Kwailing Aladdin!

Sung Din And he thought of his mother all the time, bringing her back this present because she cherished and loved him so.

Kwailing (*to Aladdin*) Did you?

Sung Din It's a present from his new and influential friends, and I tell you what: these silver salvers wouldn't half fetch a penny in the market.

Aladdin They would, Mother, they would. D'you realize? We need never be poor again? There'll always be silver salvers whenever we ask for them.

Sung Din (*to her dead husband*) There! D'you hear my son speaking? All you had was a phoney brother.

Kwailing How?

Aladdin I can get them from my influential friends. I can make us rich.

Kwailing Oh, Aladdin!

Song 10: We'll Never Be Poor Again

Aladdin (*clutching a silver salver*) Here's an end to poverty and hardship,
Here's an end to hunger in the night;
At long last an end to the time that we pretend
To be happy with the poor man's plight.

There'll be no more worry for tomorrow
Like there's been since I can't remember when,
For now we'll find that the past is left behind
And we'll never be poor again.

Chorus Never again, never again,
We'll never be poor again.

Sung Din There'll be endless enviable knick-knacks,
Like a tea-gown with semi-precious stones,
And all will see that I'm now a queen bee
And the rest are just the simple drones.

Kwailing You can take your place with all around you,
The kindest, most generous of men,
Who does much good ——

Sung Din — But no more than he should——

All For we'll never be poor again.

Chorus Never again, never again,
We'll never be poor again.

Aladdin I will turn no pauper from my pathway,
I will never spurn a begging hand,
For I know for sure what it's like to be poor
And how others do not understand.

As the world we used to know is changing,
We'll be happy, all of us, and then
I'll give and I'll give for as long as I live
For I'll ——

All (*except Aladdin*) Never be poor again!
All Never again, never again.
Aladdin We'll never be poor again.

Sung Din empties the plates and salvers and gives them to Aladdin

Sung Din (*to the audience*) Please notice, this is all my idea. The silver salvers. My idea.

She exits

Scene 3

The Desert

A fire is burning

Abenazar crouches by the fire. He turns to the audience

Abenazar Back in the beastly desert seeking for wisdom again. And something tells me there's a happy-ever-after feeling coming up in China, which I'll have to put a stop to. (*He throws some powder on the fire*) Tell me! What's happened to my lamp? (*He throws some more powder on and makes magical signs with his hands*) Tell me! (*He throws *a great dollop of powder on to the fire and makes more signs over it*) Damn well tell me!

The mysterious female voice comes from off stage

Voice The lamp is still in China.
Abanazar I know that! Where?
Voice The boy you abandoned, Aladdin ——
Abenazar He's nicked it! I left him that ring, didn't I, and that half-baked genie.
Voice Yes.
Abenazar Idiot! Utter fool!
Voice So he's rich, and maybe he'll marry a beautiful girl, and become famous and powerful and one of the most ——
Abenazar (*kicking the fire out*) Shut up! Shut up! Shut up! All that could've been mine! That snivelling little guttersnipe, I worked for those things, and they're mine, all mine—— (*He hurts his foot*) Oh, my foot! Well, I'll go back to China, now, and I'll get that lamp somehow, and —— (*singing , quickly and angrily*)

You'll all say you adore me
In a sweet harmonious tone
As I make this lousy universe
This snivelling, drivelling universe,
This deeply hateful universe,
My own, my own, my absolutely own, yes!

(*Speaking*) Beautiful girls at his age. Hah!

He exits

Scene 4

The Royal Palace

The Emperor is marching up and down. The Princess is tied to the throne, guarded by the Grand Vizier with a sword; Mrs Vizier and the two Inscrutable Ladies stand nervously nearby. Rowloon, his eyes closed, is also present

Emperor (*to the Princess*) What d'you mean, you want a bath?
Princess I want a bath.

Emperor I haven't had a bath in my life and no-one's complained.

First Inscrutable Lady
Second Inscrutable Lady } (*together*) No indeed.

Emperor Do I need a bath, Grand Vizier? (*He shoves his armpit in the Grand Vizier's face*)

Grand Vizier (*choking*) Of course not, Your Majesty.

Emperor There, you see. Baths are not necessary, which is why the palace doesn't have any.

Princess Well, I'm not going to marry Rowloon unless I have at least one bath a week between now and my wedding.

Emperor You'll marry who you're told to marry, and you're not to make me cry again!

Rowloon Since I can't look at her, it would be nice if she smelt pretty.

Emperor You can hold your nose.

First Inscrutable Lady The perfect marriage.

Second Inscrutable Lady Eyes shut ——

First Inscrutable Lady Holding your nose ——

Rowloon Mother and Father wash every week in the public baths, and they think it's ——

The Grand Vizier kicks Rowloon

Ow!

Emperor What?

Grand Vizier (*to Rowloon*) Shush!

Rowloon Well, you do, every week, with a stripey towel and soap.

First Inscrutable Lady
Second Inscrutable Lady } (*together*) Horrors!

Rowloon It's nice, I go too.

Emperor I thought you were supposed to be suitable.

Mrs Vizier He is! He is!

Princess So if he can go to the public baths, so can I!

Emperor Never! I'll chop your head off if you try!

Grand Vizier Yes! (*He draws his sword*)

Second Inscrutable Lady Quite right.

First Inscrutable Lady That'll teach her.

Princess Well — you've heard my terms.

Emperor Oh! Oh!

Rowloon So do let her go and have a bath.

Grand Vizier She'll meet people again!

Princess Go on. Let me have a bath, go on, go on.

The Princess appeals to the audience. Rowloon joins in rather enthusiastically

Emperor Stop it! Silence! Your son's opened his eyes and become a rebel.
Rowloon I just want a clean wife. Please?
Emperor (*gazing nervously at the audience*) Well, to prevent civil unrest, all right —— (*quickly*) but on one condition! That she goes alone, and that no-one, absolutely no-one, opens their eyes throughout the whole proceedings.
Mrs Vizier All right. We'll see to that. Put your sword away and look cheerful.
Grand Vizier We're always doing that.
Princess Oh, Daddy, let me hug you. (*She tries to hug the Emperor*)
Rowloon (*untying her*) Super!
Mrs Vizier (*to the Inscrutable Ladies*) Smile. And guard her like dragons.

Song 11: I'll Love You Darling Daddy When I'm Clean

Princess I'm going to bathe in the public baths
And splish and splash in lather.
When the bubbles foam up around me
I will bless my loving father.
I'll glow, I'll gleam, I'll glitter
As the brightest girl he's seen,
And I'll love you, darling Daddy, when I'm clean.
Others When she's clean.
Princess When I'm clean
Others When she's clean
Princess When I'm clean
Others When she's clean
Princess I will glisten with an alabaster sheen
Rubbed by loofahs, and I've got 'em,
When I'm scrubbed from top to bottom
I will love you, darling Daddy, when I'm clean.
Others When she's clean.
Princess My toes will twiddle the golden taps,
I'll chase the soap with pleasure,
I'll dabble and duck like a porpoise,
My limbs will stretch at leisure.

I'll sing out to my heart's content, a happy future queen,
And I'll love you darling Daddy, when I'm clean.

Others When she's clean,
Princess When I'm clean,
Others When she's clean,
Princess When I'm clean,
Others When she's clean.
Emperor As the sponges go all round and in between
Princess After this immense cascade of
Water you'll see what I'm made of
And I'll love you, darling Daddy, when I'm clean.
Others When she's clean.
Princess (*reflectively*) I'll lie all soft and comfy
And dream as the water's cooling
Of the lovely day I spent out there
In laughter, games and fooling.
I'll smile and ponder wistfully
About what might have been,
And I'll love somebody, Daddy, when I'm clean.
Others When she's clean,
Princess When I'm clean,
Others When she's clean,
Princess When I'm clean.
Others And the water's turned a nasty greyish green
She'll emerge all soft and hazy
Fresh as any country daisy
And she'll love her darling Daddy
When she's clean, clean, clean.
Princess And I'll love my darling Daddy when I'm clean!

Emperor (*speaking*) Now, make the announcement. It's lotus position time for the rest of us.

A front-cloth comes in and the two Inscrutable Ladies move forward to make the following announcement

First Inscrutable Lady
Second Inscrutable Lady } (*together, reciting*)

Citizens of the most ancient city in China, hear the words of the Emperor,

Shortly to be pinned up in a beautiful poster surrounded by dragons painted in tempera.

The Crown Princess is shortly to have a bath in the public facilities,
So we don't want anyone taking a peek at her, or any other childish imbecilities.

If they do peek, they will lose their heads and die in high disgrace,
And let us make it clear that by peek, we mean a quick and crafty look, and not that funny little dog with the pushed-in face.

Thank you.

They exit

SCENE 5

The Market

The First Merchant is sweeping out his shop

Enter Aladdin, carrying a salver, with Sung Din and Kwailing

Sung Din It's my idea, so I'll do it.
Aladdin They're my plates, so I'll do it.
Sung Din All right, all right.
Kwailing Good luck.
Sung Din I shall cover every shelf in *objets d'art*, and rare things brought from distant lands by brave middle-aged men.
Aladdin (*to the First Merchant, in a very "grown up" voice*) Good-morning.

The First Merchant bows low

Are you interested in buying a silver salver by any chance?
First Merchant We hear your uncle is not your uncle, but a robber.
Aladdin This has nothing to do with my uncle! I have more of these, and they're mine.
First Merchant More?

Kwailing A few.
Sung Din Hundreds.
Aladdin Mother!
First Merchant Then here are ten golden yen.
Aladdin Wow!
Sung Din (*shoving the salver at the First Merchant*) Take it. I'll get the rest.

Sung Din exits

Kwailing Ten golden yen!
Aladdin I'll get a new dress for you and a hat forMother and —— (*He sees something off stage*) —Oh, look out!

The Grand Vizier, Mrs Vizier and Rowloon enter. Rowloon is eating chocolates. The other Merchants enter from their shops

Grand Vizier I'll stick up these notices about the Princess's bath and ——
Mrs Vizier Then we can have a quick look round the shops.
Rowloon (*to Mrs Vizier, indicating Aladdin*) Mother, this is the horrid boy who stole my sweets and put pebbles in them.
Mrs Vizier Oh, really? Would you like to apologize?
Aladdin No. I can buy my own sweets now.
Kwailing He's a man of influence.
Aladdin I don't think we need to stay with common people.
Kwailing Let's go.
Rowloon I'm not common! I'm suitable! And my wife's going to be fragrant!

Aladdin and Kwailing move to exit

Grand Vizier Hilda, look at this salver.
Mrs Vizier Where?

Aladdin and Kwailing turn to watch

Grand Vizier Useful for the sherry and prawn crackers, don't you think?
Mrs Vizier How much is it, Mr — er ——?

The First Merchant bows deeply and does not straighten up. Mrs Vizier bows in return, somewhat perfunctorily

First Merchant (*quietly, without rising from the bow*) A hundred golden yen to the Grand Vizier's wife.

Aladdin A hundred?

Kwailing The thief!

Aladdin Wait.

Rowloon That's cheap. Next door—— (*He turns to the Second and Third Merchants*)

The Second and Third Merchants bow deeply

(*Bowing perfunctorily to the Second and Third Merchants*) — good-morning — they're going for two hundred and thirty.

Kwailing You've been cheated!

Second Merchant (*still bowing*) He's undercutting us.

Third Merchant (*also still bowing*) Sucking up to the palace.

Sung Din enters with more salvers

Sung Din Right. Get in there and buy me my dreams.

Aladdin I will. (*He takes the salvers*) Gentlemen.

The Merchants bow to Aladdin. He does not bow in return

What am I offered for each of these?

Rowloon Good heavens.

First Merchant Seventy?

Aladdin shakes his head

Second Merchant Ninety?

Aladdin shakes his head again

Third Merchant A hundred?

Aladdin sighs and turns to leave

Sung Din Aladdin, are you mad?

Kwailing Take it.

Third Merchant Ah hum! They are actually worth two hundred golden yen each. Wholesale. I'll have them. (*He holds out a bag of money*)

Aladdin (*taking the bag*) Six hundred golden yen! How about that!

Grand Vizier Amazing.

Song 12: I Got The Price I Asked For

Aladdin
Oh, I got the price I asked for and
A very nice price it *was*, you saw
I didn't bat an eyelid, simply
Didn't give an inch be*cause* I've grown so
Terribly bold and so much older
Than I used to *be*, before I
Asked for the price that was ever so nice
And made them give it *me* !

Others
Oh, see what a wise young man he is
A bargainer for all he's *worth*, oh, yes,
He's clearly a man of substance, also
Probably of noble *birth*, because we
Usually say that if you pay a price
That's horr-en-*dous*, why surely
There is a lad who cannot be bad
Because he's one of *us*.

Aladdin Oh I got the price I asked for ——
Others A bargainer for all he's worth, oh yes ——
Aladdin I just didn't bat an eye-lid ——
Others Probably of noble birth, because we ——
Aladdin Terribly bold and so much older
Than I used to be ——
I asked for the price without their advice
And made-them-give-it-me!

All (*speaking*) Well done!

Kwailing Oh Aladdin, you're wonderful!

First Merchant Any time you want our services ——

Second Merchant Anything we can do——

Third Merchant A true merchant.

Rowloon He seems rather pushy to me.

Abenazar appears in the audience

Abenazar (*to the audience*) He seems very pushy to me. Let's see what else he gets up to with my lamp — *my* lamp.

He exits

Gongs sound suddenly

Grand Vizier Ah, the Princess is going to bathe in the public baths! Eyes closed everyone, no peeking — Pekin, haha — Silence! Everyone shut their eyes!
Aladdin I don't think I feel like taking orders now.The Princess is said to be gorgeous so I think I'll find out if she is. (*He hides*)

The two Inscrutable Ladies enter with little bells, the Princess behind them, her head covered by aveil

First Inscrutable Lady Eyes terribly closed.
Second Inscrutable Lady Heads off if not.
Rowloon Hallooo! It's meeee!
Princess Eyes open, Rowloon?
Rowloon Of course not.
Princess Pity.

The procession heads towards the opposite exit

Aladdin I recognized that voice.
First Inscrutable Lady Everybody off the streets please.
Second Inscrutable Lady Including members of the Royal Household.
Grand Vizier Even me?
First Inscrutable Lady
Second Inscrutable Lady } (*together*) Horrors!

Everyone except the Princess , Aladdin and the two Inscrutable Ladies exits

Aladdin emerges from his hiding place

Aladdin Is that — is that you?

Princess Aladdin! Oh, thank goodness! (*To the Ladies*) You two, you get off the streets as well.
First Inscrutable Lady But we're supposed to guard you.
Princess Off, or I'll tell my father you played with boys.
First Inscrutable Lady
Second Inscrutable Lady } (*together*) Oh!

The two Ladies head for the exit

First Inscrutable Lady Makes you sick.

The Ladies exit

Princess There. We're alone.
Aladdin Yes.

The Princess lifts her veil and is revealed in her royal and remarkable beauty. Aladdin looks amazed

Princess Hallo. Oh, I'd forgotten how you look.
Aladdin You look amazingly — unbelievably — overwhelmingly different.
Princess Worse?
Aladdin Oh, no! Much better.

Song 13: A Girl Like This

At some point during the song, Abenazar enters and takes up a position in the audience

(*Singing*) I didn't see before
A girl like this.
I wasn't looking for
A girl like this.
I never felt so weak
And yet so very strong
Or knew a place where
I so wanted to belong.
I didn't know before
How much I care,

I wasn't ready for you standing there.
I never thought
That there could be
A person in
This world for me,
A girl, a proper girl,
Who looks like this.

Princess I didn't see before
A boy like this,
I wasn't looking for
A boy like this.
I never told myself
I thought so much of you,
Or that I loved you so,
And I already knew.
I didn't think I'd stand
In such a daze,
And long to hold your hand
And simply gaze.
I didn't see,
With open eyes,
So there you are
To my surprise,
A boy, a proper boy
Who looks like this.

Aladdin
Princess } I didn't think
Someone would say
They felt the same
Astounding way,
But here we are,
A proper girl,
A proper boy
Who looks like this.

They kiss sweetly

Abenazar She should be mine! She should be mine! It makes me furious, and I'll get him!
Aladdin (*to the Princess*) Will you marry me?

Princess I've got to have a bath.
Aladdin After that?
Princess Oh yes. Oh! I'm going to marry Rowloon, and he's so suitable.
Aladdin So am I, tremendously suitable. I'll speak to your father.
Princess He'll chop your head off.
Aladdin Don't you worry. I'll fix it.
Princess Goodness, I must go — where are those maids of mine?

The two Inscrutable Ladies enter

The Princess replaces her veil and Aladdin covers his eyes

Princess Come on, the bath will be cold before I start.
First Inscrutable Lady Don't blame us!
Princess (*to Aladdin*) Bye.
Aladdin Bye.

The Princess exits with the two Inscrutable Ladies. Rowloon, the Grand Vizier, Mrs Vizier, Sung Din and Kwailing enter

Rowloon Has she gone?
Aladdin Yes, it's all clear.
Grand Vizier And I think there's been some monkey business.
Mrs Vizier Don't use coarse expressions, dear, it makes you lemon faced.
Kwailing You peeked. Something terrible's going to happen.
Sung Din Terrible things don't happen to people like us.
Mrs Vizier Pity.
Aladdin Everything's wonderful. Mother, come with me. I need your powers of persuasion.
Sung Din Ooh. We're going up, I know it.

Aladdin and Sung Din exit

Mrs Vizier Pushy, like her son.
Rowloon (*to Kwailing*) May I say you're quite nice in a common sort of manner?
Kwailing I'm rather upset, actually.
Rowloon (*comfortingly*) Aaah.
Mrs Vizier Rowloon. You should be through your shop-girl phase by now.
Rowloon I don't know what you mean.

All but Mrs Vizier exit; possibly a front-cloth could come down

Abenazar (*coming out of the audience*) Excuse me, dear lady.
Mrs Vizier Yes?
Abenazar I can't help noticing a little worry here: your boy heading downmarket, and a young upstart planning to marry the Princess ——
Mrs Vizier What?
Abenazar They were smooching. I saw.
Mrs Vizier You mean that boy with the pebbles?
Abenazar I'm afraid so. Just let them have their way for a bit, and they'll make some ghastly mistake. And then I'll be at hand to help you. Trust me.

Abenazar exits smiling

Mrs Vizier That hooligan and his appalling mother won't spoil my future. I may be called Hilda, but I intend to be an Emperor's mother-in-law. *(She calls into the wings)* Thank you very much!

Mrs Vizier exits

Scene 6

The Royal Palace

The Emperor is seated on his throne. The Grand Vizier, Mrs Vizier, the two Inscrutable Ladies, the Princess and Rowloon are present. The room is full of gifts

Emperor Have I received all today's presents from our poor and humble citizens?
Grand Vizier There's one more, Your Majesty, though she's not exactly poor.
Mrs Vizier And certainly not humble.
Emperor Promising. Send her in.
Grand Vizier Mrs Din, please.
Emperor What a noisy name — Din. Ha ha. (*He chortles*)

The two Inscrutable Ladies laugh as well; the others are silent

Heads may roll if I'm not appreciated.

Sung Din enters wearing an expensive dress

Sung Din (*to the audience*) I've only gone and got a tea-gown, haven't I. I've arrived, you see, top of the pile and just watch this. (*To the Emperor*) So you're the Emperor, are you?
Emperor Of course.
Grand Vizier Bow low.
Sung Din I'm Sung Din, daughter of a Mandarin. And my son Aladdin wants to marry your daughter.
Grand Vizier No!
Princess Yes.
Mrs Vizier No!
Grand Vizier No!
Rowloon No!
Emperor Certainly not!
Rowloon He's horrid!
Princess He's lovely!
Emperor How d'you know?
Princess I met him out there.
Emperor Well, people lose their heads for meeting you, so have him put in prison.
Sung Din Just one minute, Emperor cock. I've got some jewels for you, if you're interested.
Grand Vizier He's not.
Emperor I might be.
Sung Din Kwailing!
Grand Vizier Blast it.

Kwailing enters pulling a loaded and covered cart, muttering to herself

Kwailing I don't want to do this, I don't know why I'm doing it, I'm losing the best person in the world again ——
Rowloon Oh, hallo.
Mrs Vizier Keep your distance, boy.
Sung Din Now, Your Majesty, look at these little gems, which go so well with the décor. (*She pulls a cloth off the cart, revealing the jewel fruits from the cave, which glow beautifully*)
Emperor Oh! Oh, my goodness, Grand Vizier, look at them.

Mrs Vizier (*to the audience*) I'll bet that's magic, and that's against the law.
Emperor (*fondling the jewels*) Where did they come from?
Sung Din My son.
Emperor Can you do that?
Princess No, so come on, Father, say yes to Aladdin.
Rowloon No!
Grand Vizier No!
Kwailing No!
Rowloon Quite.
Kwailing I want him.
Sung Din You can't have him.
Grand Vizier You promised the Princess to us.
Emperor But I want the jewels.
Mrs Vizier Your Majesty, I wonder if I could just have a word about the laws against magic ——
Grand Vizier Don't interfere.
Sung Din You can't have the jewels unless you say yes to the wedding of your daughter to my son, so think.
First Inscrutable Lady What a problem.
Second Inscrutable Lady Oh dear.
Grand Vizier Let us try the well-known forty day solution, Your Majesty. If in forty days this lady's son can produce forty times as many of these baubles, so much less important than true love, of course, then he can marry the Princess. If not, he loses his head.
Mrs Vizier If he does produce them, of course, he could be doing magic which ——
Grand Vizier Leave the plotting to me.
Emperor Can he produce more?
Princess For me he can do anything.
Kwailing Oh, you fantasy figures ——
Sung Din And if he does, they'll be married on the spot?
Princess Yes.
Kwailing
Rowloon } (*together*) No.
Mrs Vizier If he does, he'll certainly be using magic, so ——
Emperor Right. But I must keep these now, non-returnable.
Sung Din Done. Come along, Kwailing, we've managed it.
Grand Vizier See them out, Rowloon.
Kwailing That bossy princess, it's only because she's had a bath.

Sung Din, Kwailing and Rowloon enter

Emperor I don't see how I can lose, Grand Vizier. I've got these, I might get more, and if I don't, you get my daughter. I'm so glad you went to the public baths.

Grand Vizier But ——

Emperor Oh, there's always a but, isn't there?

Grand Vizier You promised the Princess to Rowloon, come what may.

Mrs Vizier Yes.

Grand Vizier And if the word gets about that you broke your promise just to get some jewels, people might say "What a naughty Emperor! He must have his head cut off."

Mrs Vizier Oh! Yes, yes, yes.

First Inscrutable Lady }
Second Inscrutable Lady } (*together*) Yes!

Princess Rubbish!

Grand Vizier They might. All your humble citizens love Rowloon.

Mrs Vizier They do.

First Inscrutable Lady }
Second Inscrutable Lady } (*together*) Because he's suitable!

Song 14: He's Suitable, He's Suitable

Grand Vizier }
Mrs Vizier }
Ladies }

He's suitable, he's suitable
You promised her to him,
His views are quite immutable
So loyal, true and dim.
You've always said you'd give us her
To make the crown our own.
You can't go back, so we aver,
Unless you lose your throne.
Don't look so lost and helpless for
You must do what you said
And if you dither, possibly,
You'll lose your royal head.
He's suitable.

Emperor (*speaking*) He is, and I did promise. Oh, dear.

Grand Vizier Act quickly. Marry the Princess and Rowloon today. (*He indicates the jewels*) You'll still have these.

Princess No!

Mrs Vizier Yes! (*To the audience*) Then if Aladdin uses magic to get her back, we can chop his head off.

Song 14A: He's Suitable, He's Suitable (Reprise)

Grand Vizier
Mrs Vizier
Ladies } He's suitable, he's suitable,
You know his breeding tells
He'll never come home newtable
Or gaze on other gels.
Although it could be trying if
He chattered all day long,
Consider, as he bores you stiff
His health is none too strong.

Emperor (*speaking: heading towards the exit*) All right. She shall marry Rowloon. Take her away and prepare her for a wedding this very morning.

Mrs Vizier (*to the audience*) Now let's see if Aladdin is trying to be clever.

The Emperor sweeps off with the Grand Vizier. Mrs Vizier and the Inscrutable Ladies force the Princess towards the exit

Princess (*to the audience*) Call Aladdin! Tell him what's happening!

The audience is encouraged to call for Aladdin

The Princess, Mrs Vizier and the Inscrutable Ladies exit

Aladdin and Sung Din enter

Aladdin What is it? Married to Rowloon? I'll put a pretty quick stop to that.

Sung Din You'd better. I've ordered the crested notepaper.

Aladdin Here we go. (*He produces the lamp and rubs it*)

There is the sound of thunder; mist and magical lighting effects fill the stage

The Genie of the Lamp appears as before

Genie of the Lamp What is your wish?
Aladdin I wish to marry the Crown Princess, whom I love, at the wedding the Emperor is planning.
Genie of the Lamp To hear is to obey.
Sung Din And when you've done that, just build us all a beautiful palace to live in, will you?
Aladdin An excellent idea, Mother.
Genie of the Lamp When the time comes, clap your hands and it will be done. Farewell.

The Genie disappears and the throne room returns to normal

Aladdin When the time comes! Now let it work.
Sung Din And the palace was another of my ideas, please notice. My idea, the palace.

Aladdin and Sung Din exit

The Princess is brought in by the two Inscrutable Ladies. She is wearing a wedding dress, her hands are chained behind her and her mouth is gagged. Rowloon, the Grand Vizier and Mrs Vizier enter too. All except Rowloon and the Princess sing the next reprise of the song, which has a more solemn version of the tune

Song 14B: He's Suitable, He's Suitable (Reprise)

All
He's suitable, he's suitable,
He's quite the best in town,
He's probably quite bootable
Upstairs and then back down.
So take your vows, and do not heed
The feelings of despair,
Your married life can just proceed
As if he were not there.

Emperor Let's get on with it. Wedding of the Crown Princess of China to Rowloon the Suitable. Rowloon, do you take this girl to be your lawfully wedded wife?

Rowloon Well, I don't want to take her if she's going to boot me ——

Emperor That's a yes. Daughter, do you take Rowloon the Suitable to be your lawfully wedded husband?

Princess (*spitting out the gag*) No!

There is a loud crash, a flash and a cloud of smoke. Rowloon disappears shouting "Help!". There is another crash, another flash and Sung Din, Aladdin and the Genie of the Ring appear, with Aladdin taking over the place previously occupied by Rowloon. The Genie carries a large suitcase

Emperor What on earth — who the dickens ——

Princess Oh Aladdin! You really are remarkable!

Aladdin Yes, I am.

Mrs Vizier He's using magic. Arrest him!

Sung Din Oh why don't you shut your bleeding great cake-hole?

Genie of the Ring Who ordered jewels?

Emperor Me!

Genie of the Ring Here they are and have a banana. (*She produces a banana magically*) And get marrying!

Mrs Vizier It's magic! It is not allowed!

Emperor Grand Vizier?

Grand Vizier I'm sorry, Your Majesty, I'm looking for my son. Rowloon?

Mrs Vizier Where's that man?

Abenazar (*from the audience*) Don't worry, dear lady, our time will come.

Sung Din Well — er — do you take ——

Princess
Aladdin } (*together*) Yes!

Song 14C: He's Suitable, He's Suitable (Reprise)

All

And that is very clearly that,
Rowloon has now been ditched,
And here's long life to man and wife
And long may they stay hitched!

Emperor (*speaking*) But where d'you think you're going to live?

Aladdin Oh, now this really will surprise you. Out in the garden, of course! (*He claps his hands*)

The scene magically changes into the new palace, which is liberally piled with cushions

Sung Din Well, how about that?
Mrs Vizier I have to say, loudly, this is magic and against the law.
First Inscrutable Lady It is!
Second Inscrutable Lady It is!
Emperor No. It's amazing!
Princess You're more than remarkable. You're superb.
Aladdin And so are you.
Sung Din Just a minute. This was my idea.
Aladdin Yes, well——
Sung Din A home fit for the daughter of a Mandarin. Look, you royals, my very own personal triumph!

Song 15: With Grit and Gumption

(*Singing*)

I've seen the best, I've seen the worst,
I've been let down by wicked uncles.
Now at last I've come up first,
And I've got jewels like carbuncles,
Pillared doors, and knobs of brass,
A vast expanse of plated glass,
And you'll recall I did it all
With grit and gumption.

I've struggled down life's rotten road
And suffered vast humiliations.
Now my dinner plates are Spode
With very fancy decorations,
And chiffon drapes, a bed of silk,
And baths, I hope, in asses' milk;
Oh, what a ball, I did it all
With grit and gumption.

I've fought the fight, I've won the war,
And got at last my parquet floor.
Oh, what a ball, I did it all
With grit and gumption.

The Grand Vizier rearranges some cushions and discovers Rowloon and Kwailing under them

Mrs Vizier (*shrieking*) Aaah! What's all this?
Rowloon We were just sitting in the garden, picking flowers ——
Kwailing And feeling very sorry for ourselves ——
Rowloon When whoosh, this blooming great palace came rushing down ——
Kwailing And landed right on top of us.
Rowloon Am I to finish marrying the Princess now?
Aladdin No. She's married to me. (*To the Emperor*) Let me show you round, Father-in-law.
Sung Din Desirable neighbourhood, garden laid to lawn, worth a bob or two, eh?

The Emperor, the Princess, Sung Din, Aladdin and the Inscrutable Ladies exit

Mrs Vizier Everything's gone wrong! Man! Man! Hasn't our time come yet?
Abenazar (*from the orchestra*) Nearly. Just be patient.
Grand Vizier You're talking to yourself, my dear, and that's a bad sign.

The front-cloth comes in; Kwailing and Rowloon move in front of it

Kwailing I'm miserable.
Rowloon So am I.

Song 16 : When Everybody's Happy But You

Kwailing

When everybody's happy
But you.
Very merry, very snappy
But you.
There's a gnawing little feeling
That is very unappealing
In your tummy and it's spiteful,
So unpositive and frightful
That you really can't believe
It's true
That everybody's happy but you.

It's got to stop,
It drives you mad.
Life's far too good
To feel this bad.

But when everybody's happy
But you.
There's nothing, no there's nothing
You can do.

Rowloon When everybody's loving
But you,
Footy-footing, lovey-doving
But you,
There's something very rotten
In the feeling you're forgotten,
Makes you miserable and mouldy,
Like a far-from-golden oldie
That everybody's happy but you.

It has to end,
You know it must,
Life isn't only
Rust and dust.

So when everyone is loving
But you
There's nothing, no there's nothing
You can do.

Dance break

Both It's got to stop
It drives you mad,
Life's far too good
To feel this bad.

But when everybody's loving but you,
There's nothing, no there's nothing,

No there's nothing, no there's nothing,
No there's nothing, no there's nothing,
You can do, boo hoo!
I'm glad you feel the same way too.

They exit together

Scene 7

Abenazar appears in the audience. He is disguised, with a basket of lamps

Abenazar New lamps for old! New lamps for —— (*He reveals himself to the audience*) It's me, and I saw all that and I am seething with rage, very nearly out of control, and now the time has come for my revenge! New lamps for old! New bloody lamps! This is my trick to get the other lamp for myself, you'll see, because it's mine, mine — and don't you ever feel like that, eh, when people have the things that should be yours? Doesn't it make you really, really mad? Doesn't it make you want to shout YABOO! It makes me want to scrawl all over the walls of the palace and throw bricks through the windows and mess up the flower beds and puke on the gravel paths — Yaboo! Yaboo! Yaboo!

The front-cloth rises to reveal the outside of a window in the new palace

The Princess can be seen in the window, performing some domestic task such as flower arranging. The Inscrutable Ladies, as maids, are standing watching her

Abenazar approaches from the audience

(*Suddenly sweet*) New lamps for old, new lamps for old.
Princess Who's that?
First Inscrutable Lady It's a man offering something new for something old.
Second Inscrutable Lady He must be mad.
First Inscrutable Lady Mad.
Second Inscrutable Lady Mad.

They both laugh

Abenazar comes to the window

Abenazar Oh! What a pretty lady!

Princess What's this "New lamps for old"?

Abenazar I collect antiques, dear. Yesterday's things are so much better than today's, don't you think?

Princess No, actually.

Abenazar Then let me give you a new lamp to light your pretty life, eh? That is, if you have an old one to — er — er ——

First Inscrutable Lady There's one in the master's study, Your Highness.

Second Inscrutable Lady Really smelly and nasty.

First Inscrutable Lady
Second Inscrutable Lady } (*together*) He won't let us touch it.

Abenazar A nice modern palace like this, you don't want a horrid old thing littering it up, hm?

Princess Go and fetch it, will you?

The two Inscrutable Ladies exit

Abenazar Your husband out, is he?

Princess At the market.

Abenazar So choose a lovely, bright lamp as a surprise for him. (*He holds up the basket so that she can see the lamps*)

Princess (*indicating a lamp*) This one's quite nice.

Abenazar (*pulling the lamp from the basket*) And we just need yours, of course.

The two Inscrutable Ladies enter with Aladdin's lamp

First Inscrutable Lady
Second Inscrutable Lady } (*together*) Here we are.

The Inscrutable Ladies hand Aladdin's lamp to Abenazar in exchange for the new lamp

Abenazar There! (*Gleefully*) There!

Abenazar exits, leaving his basket behind

Princess (*taking the new lamp*) It really is new. It's a funny sort of exchange. (*She sees the basket of lamps*) Oh. (*Calling off*) You've left these!
Abenazar (*off*) Keep them till we meet again! (*He laughs madly*)
Princess Actually, I rather hope we don't.

Sung Din enters

Sung Din Do we have one of those baths that squirts at you in unexpected places and —— (*Indicating the basket of lamps*) Oh! What's that?
Second Inscrutable Lady We exchanged it for ——
First Inscrutable Lady }
Second Inscrutable Lady } (*together*) The master's old lamp!
Sung Din You didn't! Get it back. Everything that matters to us is in that lamp.

A faint rumble comes from off stage. We hear the distant voice of the Genie of the Lamp

Genie of the Lamp (*off*) What is your wish?
Sung Din Oh. Too late ...
Genie of the Lamp (*off*) To hear is to obey!
Princess Too late? I really don't know what you're ——

We hear thunder, crashes, bangs and whistling sounds fading into the distance; darkness falls rapidly, punctuated by lightning

Scene 8

A Garden

The Lights come up to reveal the Emperor, the Grand Vizier and Mrs Vizier standing together. The Emperor has his hand raised as if he is about to knock on a door

Emperor There was a palace here just now. I was going to knock on the door.

Mrs Vizier I knew it! That boy has spirited your daughter away.
Grand Vizier Then he's doing magic——
Mrs Vizier At last!
Grand Vizier — and magic ——
Emperor — is illegal!
Grand Vizier And therefore wicked.
Mrs Vizier And people who practise it have their heads cut off. So Aladdin has to die, and the Princess will need a new husband.
Grand Vizier
Mrs Vizier } (*together*) Rowloon!
Mrs Vizier Lovely.

Aladdin enters

Aladdin What's happened?
Emperor You! You know what's happened. You've taken away my daughter ——
Grand Vizier By magic ——
Emperor By magic — And I'm heartbroken, so chop his head off, Grand Vizier, now! So I feel better!
Grand Vizier (*drawing his sword*) Yes.
Aladdin (*falling to his knees*) I swear to you that I know nothing of this disaster, and my heart is broken just as much as yours.
Emperor A likely tale.
Mrs Vizier (*to the Grand Vizier*) Get chopping, dear.
Emperor Yes!

Rowloon and Kwailing enter

Rowloon Father, I want to get married.
Grand Vizier Wait a second.
Kwailing You mustn't do that.
Aladdin Kwailing, the palace has disappeared and my lovely princess with it.
Emperor Hurry up.
Aladdin It must've been Uncle Abenazar.
Kwailing (*to the audience*) Was it?

The audience is encouraged to answer "Yes"

Then Aladdin mustn't die, must he?

The audience is encouraged to answer "No"

So — let him go, let him go, let him go.

Kwailing encourages the audience to join in with "Let him go"

Emperor Silence! (*He moves to face Kwailing*) You are causing civil unrest.
Kwailing Yes! Let him go.
Rowloon Oh, you are strong, Kwailing.
Kwialing Yes, so I am.
Emperor Grand Vizier, put that away. I can't stand revolutions. I'll let you go on one condition, Aladdin. The forty day solution.
Grand Vizier Oh bother.
Emperor For forty days and nights you will go and search for my daughter and do everything you can to bring her back. If you don't succeed, the Grand Vizier here will chop your head off. All right?
Aladdin Yes.
Emperor And you'll try very hard?
Aladdin Of course.
Emperor Good, because I love her so much. (*He cries*) Lotus position, then, till you get back.

The Emperor exits

The Grand Vizier and Mrs Vizier move to follow him

Grand Vizier (*to Aladdin*) Trickster.
Mrs Vizier We'll get you, just you see. (*She beckons to Rowloon*) Rowloon!

The Grand Vizier and Mrs Vizier exit

Kwailing You will find her won't you.
Aladdin I just don't know where to start.
Rowloon We want to get married.

Rowloon exits

Aladdin (*calling*) Princess? Princess, where are you? (*He stamps his foot*) Oh! I'm just like they all said, no good at anything. (*He becomes tearful and puts his hands to his eyes. He feels the ring*) The ring! Oh, the ring! (*He rubs the ring*)

There is a flash

The Genie of the Ring enters

Genie of the Ring Now it's no use hoping for a miracle, love, because you know quite well it's only the tricks with me.
Aladdin Do you know where the Princess is, then?
Genie of the Ring She's off in the African desert, I'm afraid, with that uncle in the new palace which he got with the lamp which he stole, so let's sit down and play dominoes, shall we?
Aladdin But Abenazar's cruel. Can't you get me there?
Genie of the Ring Well, I could try, if you really don't like dominoes.
Aladdin Yes, try.

The Genie of the Ring strains, making a "whoosh" sound

Genie of the Ring (*after a moment*) No good.
Aladdin I'll help you.

They both try, making the "whoosh" sound

(*To the audience*) Come on, you lot as well. Whoosh away.

The audience is encouraged to "whoosh"

Nearly, try again.

Aladdin, the Genie of the Ring and the audience all try again

That's it! I'm off! I'm away!

Aladdin flies skywards

Genie of the Ring Lovely! There's one or two of you out there got quite a way with magic.

Scene 9

A map flies in with a song sheet on it. On the map is a line of lights which show how Aladdin is progressing in his journey

Genie of the Ring Ah, here's a map so we can see how he's getting on. There he is, flying along here in China, and he has to get all the way over there to the African desert, where Abenazar has taken the Princess. And here — well I never — is a little song we can all sing to give him that extra bit of magic he needs to get there.

Song 17: Fly, Fly, Fly!

(*Singing*)
He's swooping!
He's soaring!
He's going to save the day!
His princess
Is calling
From very far away.
So fly hard, Aladdin,
Be master of the sky.
Your uncle's being horrible
So fly, fly, fly!

(*Speaking*) Oh, he's stuck here, in these cold and terrifying mountains, the Howling Himalayas. He can't get over! Come on, sing louder to get him to fly higher!

The song is repeated

(*Speaking*) Louder!

The song is repeated

(*Speaking*) Oh, well done, he's over, and look, he's nearly there. One more time.

The song is repeated. The lights arrive at Abenazar's desert hideaway

(*Speaking*) Some of you are really very good. I'll have to have a word with you about magic training. Now then, let's see what's happening in the desert.

Scene 10

An apartment in the new palace. Evening

A number of the lamps from Abenazar's box stand about the room, lit. A table, with wine and glasses on it stands at the back of the stage and a couch is prominent in the room. Palm trees can be seen beyond the windows; cicadas hum

The Princess and the two Inscrutable Ladies are discovered

There is a banging at a door

Abenazar (*off*) Princess, oh Princess! It's your friendly lamp seller wanting to come and talk about life and things.
Princess I'll never let you in here to talk about anything.
First Inscrutable Lady This comes of marrying a commoner.

Aladdin appears

Aladdin Princess, I've found you.
Princess Aah. Aladdin, darling, darling Aladdin, I knew you'd find me. A terrible man took away an old lamp of yours and ——
Aladdin I know.

There are several loud bangs at the door

Abenazar (*off*) I'd like to take you on a trip round the world, Princess, and bring you home for supper time and hot chocolate.
Aladdin I'll deal with him.
Abenazar Let me in, my sweetest, or I'll force my way in with my magic lamp again.
First Inscrutable Lady
Second Inscrutable Lady } (*together*) Oh!

Sung Din enters

Sung Din Do just let him have a little kiss, love, and then he'll leave us to bathe in the oasis. (*To Aladdin*) Oh! I hope you haven't come to spoil things.

Princess She's a real pain.
Aladdin I have come to spoil things.
Sung Din Well, just remember what happened last time you upset him, that's all. (*She speaks to the ground*) It's your son stirring it up again.
Aladdin Out, go on, out.
Sung Din What?
Aladdin (*to the Inscrutable Ladies*) And you, please. It won't be long.

Everyone except Aladdin and the Princess head for the exit

First Inscrutable Lady Isn't he strong?

They exit

Aladdin Now, there's no magic I can use. You'll have to trust me.
Princess I do.
Aladdin Then let Abenazar in and offer him some wine. Go over to the table to get it, and don't turn back until I tell you. Now. (*He rolls up his sleeve and hides*)
Abenazar (*off*) I'm going to count to ten and then I'm going to ——

The Princess opens the door

Ah!

Abenazar enters

How very, very lovely. You do know, don't you, that we're going to live in this desert for ever so we ought to be friends, don't you think?
Princess Would you like some wine?
Abenazar I would love some wine, lots and lots of wine.

The Princess moves to the back of the stage to pour out the wine. Abenazar reclines on the couch

Oh, the joy of it all, ruling things from our little oasis, dreaming up new games and ——

Aladdin comes out of hiding

Dear boy, I hope you haven't misunderstood anything I've done. It's all been for you, if I can just think of a way to explain it. Why don't you come to my arms to be nurtured, eh?
Aladdin I want the lamp.

Abenazar stands and opens his arms. We see that he has a knife concealed. Aladdin moves to Abenazar, who moves to stab him. They wrestle; during the struggle Abenazar falls on his knife and screams

Abenazar (*hiding his face*) You swine! You little guttersnipe! (*He sings*) "You deprived and fatherless boy". (*To the audience*) I should've chosen one of you. (*He staggers towards the exit*) Don't think evil can be got rid of so easily. When you go to bed tonight, look behind the cupboard door. Watch for my little pointy shoes where the curtain meets the floor!

He exits to music

Aladdin Princess, turn around now. We're safe.
Princess I want to go home. Get me there.
Aladdin Yes. (*He calls off*) Come here, Mother, and you, girls. This may be the last magic of all.

Sung Din and the Inscrutable Ladies enter

Where's the lamp?

The Genie of the Ring appears in the audience with the lamp

Genie of the Ring (*referring to the lamp*) I got it from Abenazar's room. (*She picks two children out of the audience*) And I've had my eye on these two little people all evening, because they're the ones who've got a way with the magic. Now you two come with me, that's it, and let's have a good old rub on the lamp, shall we? (*She leads the children on to the stage*)
Princess Good.

The children rub the lamp. The Genie of the Lamp appears

Oh!

Genie of the Lamp What is your wish?
Genie of the Ring Tell him you'd like this palace to go back to China.

The children relay this wish to the Genie of the Lamp

Sung Din And — wait — I'd like to have one or two extra fittings in it, talking points, really, like a stuffed alligator, a few elephants' feet to hold umbrellas ——

There is a roll of thunder

Genie of the Lamp You ask too much! You always want more and more and more and so you shall have nothing and stay here in the desert.
Princess No, no, don't listen to her!
Aladdin No.
Genie of the Ring Oh, just let them have the one wish to get back to China, 'cause it was really these nice little people who asked.
Aladdin (*to the Genie of the Lamp*)We'll give you the lamp so we can never use it to get what we want again, especially Mother.
Genie of the Lamp You shall go home, then, but from now on — no magic.
Genie of the Ring Just a quick box of Turkish delight. (*She produces a box of Turkish delight and gives it to the children*)
Genie of the Lamp Now, throw me the lamp and you will be free.
Princess Let me do it. (*She throws the lamp through the Genie's mouth*)

There is a great deal of noise and many lighting effects as the Genie of the Lamp disappears. The Genie of the Ring brings the children back into the audience and stays with them until the effects sequence is over, saying

Genie of the Ring Quick, let's get out of here while it's safe. (*Etc.*)

Scene 11

The same palace

The scenery outside the windows is Chinese. The Grand Vizier, Mrs Vizier, Rowloon and Kwailing are discovered at the front of the stage; Sung Din, Aladdin, the Princess and the Inscrutable Ladies are crouching at the back

Rowloon (*to the Grand Vizier*)Well, we want to get married, Father, now, and if the Emperor's too unhappy to read the service, you can do it.

Kwailing. The quicker the better.

Mrs Vizier This is the most disappointing day of my life.

Grand Vizier (*surprised*) We were standing in the garden a minute ago.

Aladdin (*stepping forward*) I've done what the Emperor asked me and I shall never practise magic again, nor do anything that is not kind and gentle.

Grand Vizier He's got the blasted Princess! Your Majesty, he's got the girl!

The Emperor enters

Emperor Where is she? Where's my little sweet and sour dumpling? Put that sword away, Grand Vizier, in fact throw it away. What can I say? Is there anything in the world you would like?

Aladdin No.

Princess No.

Aladdin Unless it's this. That Rowloon and Kwailing get married straight away, and discover, like us, that there's no magic like the magic of another human being.

Song 18: Magic

Genie of the Ring
We've had a bit of trouble
With an uncle and a lamp,
But please don't think that magic
Always turns out quite so damp.
There's masses there inside you all,
Like in these couples here.

Aladdin and the Princess, Kwailing and Rowloon, kiss

Aah!
So, just before you go away,
My loves, please lend an ear.
Oh ——

Magic —
It's there with everyone
Magic —
To share with everyone.
Look inside,
Don't hide your magic away.

All Magic —
Come on and give a bit;
Magic —
Make people live a bit
Pass it round,
And around, let everyone play.

Women It makes your rainy days turn sunny
It makes your mum and dad go funny
Men It makes your teachers smile and grin a bit
All Makes all your nice friends want to sin a bit.
Choose it.
Aladdin, Princess, Rowloon, Kwailing To froth and bubble with.
All Use it.
Aladdin, Princess, Rowloon, Kwailing Although there's trouble with
All Magic, magic,
Blow your mind with it,
Magic, magic,
You will find with it,
Magic, magic makes a beautiful day.
Women Magic —
It's rather scrumptious and
Magic —
Sung Din It's big and bumptious and
Women Let's get spreading
And shedding magic around.

Aladdin
Princess } Dream it.
And love will snuggle up.

Rowloon
Kwailing } Scream it
And joy will struggle up.

Ladies Let it swing
And ring with wonderful sound.
(*They ring bells or hit gongs*)

Grand Vizier
Mrs Vizier } It makes you nice when you've been naughty

Emperor And stops you feeling high and haughty.

Abenazar It shows that success comes easily
If you smile a lot more greasily.

All Magic—
It's warm and cuddlesome—

Aladdin
Princess
Rowloon
Kwailing } Sometimes
It's awfully muddlesome.

All Magic, magic
Blow your mind with it,
Magic, magic,
You will find with it,
Magic, magic makes a beautiful day.

Dance

Women It's never just a field of clover
It gets you, grabs you, turns you over,

Men It gleams and glows in every part of you
Causing earthquakes in the heart of you.

All Choose it

Aladdin
Princess
Rowloon
Kwailing } To froth and bubble with.

All Use it.

Aladdin
Princess
Rowloon
Kwailing } Although there's trouble with

All	Magic magic, Blow your mind with it, Magic, magic, You will find with it, Magic, magic, Makes a beautiful day.
Aladdin **Princess** **Rowloon** **Kwailing**	It's great to give a bit of
All	Magic
Aladdin **Princess** **Rowloon** **Kwailing**	Make people live a bit with
All	Magic.
Aladdin **Princess** **Rowloon** **Kwailing**	Come on and give a bit of
All	Magic.
Aladdin	Makes a beautiful
Princess	Makes a beautiful
Rowloon	Makes a beautiful
Kwailing	Makes a beautiful
All	Day!

CURTAIN

FURNITURE AND PROPERTY LIST

ACT 1

Scene 1

On stage: Practical fire
Sand

Scene 2

On stage: Pebble
Off stage: Bag of chocolates (**Aladdin**)

Scene 3

Personal: **Grand Vizier**: sword (worn throughout)

Scene 4

Off stage: Swathes of cloth (**Sung Din**)
Barrow (**Aladdin**)
Personal: **Abenazar**: gold coins

Scene 5

No props

Scene 6

Off stage: Glass of sherry (**Sung Din**)
Food, including purple lollipops (**Aladdin** and **Kwailing**)
Large basket containing fruits and wines (**Servant**)

Scene 7

Off stage: Cushion, little bells (**Inscrutable Ladies**)

Personal: **Princess**: ropes

Scene 8

On stage: *In shop*: Chinese tunic, trousers and skull cap

Personal: **Abenazar**: gold coins

Scene 9

Off stage: Sweets (**Abenazar**)

Scene 10

On stage: Piles of stones and rocks in front of marble doors
Twigs

Personal: **Abenazar**: ring

Scene 11

On stage: Oil lamp
Magic jewel fruit

ACT II

Scene 1

On stage: as ACT 1 Scene 11

Off stage: Sandwich, bottle of pop, foo yong, three rabbits, birdcage with bird, row of sparklers (**Genie of the Ring**)

Scene 2

On stage: Lamp
Magic jewel fruit

Off stage: Popadam (**Genie of the Ring**)
Sumptuous meal on silver salvers (**Servants**)
Salt (**Genie of the Ring**)

SCENE 3

On stage: Practical fire

Personal: Magic powder (**Abenazar**)

SCENE 4

Personal: **Princess**: ropes

SCENE 5

Off stage: Broom (**First Merchant**)
Salver (**Aladdin**)
Chocolates (**Rowloon**)
Salvers (**Sung Din**)
Little bells (**Inscrutable Ladies**)

Personal: **Third Merchant**: bag of money

SCENE 6

On stage: Gifts

Off stage: Cart containing magic jewel fruits covered with cloth (**Kwailing**)
Banana, suitcase (**Genie of the Ring**)

Personal: **Princess**: chairs, gag

During scene change page 64:

Set: Cushions

SCENE 7

On stage: Vase of flowers

Off stage: Basket. *In it*: lamps (**Abenazar**)
Aladdin's lamp (**Inscrutable Ladies**)

SCENE 8

No props

SCENE 9

No props

SCENE 10

On stage: Lamps (*practical*)
Table. *On it*: Bottles of wine, glasses
Couch

Off stage: Aladdin's lamp, Turkish delight (**Genie of the Ring**)

Personal: **Abenazar**: knife

SCENE 11

No props

LIGHTING PLOT

Property fittings required: fire, flares, line of lights on map, lamps

Various simple interior and exterior settings

ACT I

To open: Dim light with fire glow

Cue 1 **Abenazar** throws sand on the fire (Page 1)
Flame effect

Cue 2 **Abenazar** throws sand on the fire (Page 1)
Flame effect

Cue 3 **Abenazar** throws sand on the fire (Page 1)
Flame effect

Cue 4 **Voice**: "Now leave me!" (Page 1)
Flame effect

Cue 5 **Abenazar** exits (Page 3)
Cross-fade to shop fronts: general exterior lighting

Cue 6 **Rowloon** exits (Page 6)
Cross-fade to Royal Palace: general exterior lighting

Cue 7 The **Princess** exits (Page 12)
Cross-fade to exterior of Aladdin's house

Cue 8 **Aladdin** and **Kwailing** exit (Page 16)
Cross-fade to front-cloth lighting

Cue 9 **All** exit (Page 19)
Cross-fade to interior of Aladdin's house

Cue 10 End of "Little Shop" reprise (Page 23)
Cross-fade to Royal Palace lighting

Cue 11	**All** exit *Cross-fade to dim market lighting: shops lit with flares*	(Page 26)
Cue 12	**Aladdin** exits *Lights in shops fade; bring up moonlight effect*	(Page 29)
Cue 13	**Abenazar**: "...Will be as rich as me!" *Cross-fade to town with sunrise effect*	(Page 29)
Cue 14	**Abenazar** lights the twigs *Spark effect in fire*	(Page 32)
Cue 15	Door swings open *Light beams out from cave*	(Page 33)
Cue 16	**Abenazar**: "Keep going!" *Cross-fade to cave interior lighting*	(Page 34)

ACT II

To open: General interior lights on cave

Cue 17	**Aladdin** rubs the lamp *Lights fade*	(Page 38)
Cue 18	Mist pours down *Bring up lights on giant lips*	(Page 38)
Cue 19	**Genie of the Lamp**: "To hear is to obey." *Fade lights on lips*	(Page 39)
Cue 20	Enormous wind sounds *Cross-fade to Sung Din's house: general interior lighting*	(Page 39)
Cue 21	**Sung Din**: "My idea." She exits *Cross-fade to desert lighting; fire glow on*	(Page 43)
Cue 22	**Abenazar**: "Hah!" *Cross-fade to Royal Palace lighting*	(Page 44)

Cue 23	Front-cloth comes in *Cross-fade to front-cloth lighting*	(Page 47)
Cue 24	The **Inscrutable Ladies** exit *Cross-fade to market lighting*	(Page 48)
Cue 25	**Mrs Vizier** exits *Cross-fade to Royal Palace lighting*	(Page 56)
Cue 26	**Sung Din** pulls cloth off cart *Bring up glow effect on cart*	(Page 57)
Cue 27.	**Aladdin** rubs the lamp *Magical lighting effects*	(Page 60)
Cue 28	**Aladdin** claps his hands *Cross-fade to new palace lighting*	(Page 63)
Cue 29	Front-cloth comes in *Cross-fade to front-cloth lighting*	(Page 64)
Cue 30	Front-cloth rises *Cross-fade to exterior lighting for new palace*	(Page 66)
Cue 31	**Princess**: "I really don't know what you're ——" *Fade lights rapidly with flashes of lightning*	(Page 68)
Cue 32	When ready *Bring up lights on garden*	(Page 68)
Cue 33	Map flies in *Bring up line of lights one by one as the song progresses*	(Page 72)
Cue 34	**Genie of the Ring**: " ... in the desert." *Cross-fade to new palace lighting (interior)*	(Page 72)
Cue 35	**Princess** throws lamp through Genie's mouth *Magical lighting effects*	(Page 76)
Cue 36	When ready *Cross-fade to new palace lighting (interior)*	(Page 76)

EFFECTS PLOT

ACT I

Cue 1 As CURTAIN rises (Page 1)
Wind

Cue 2 **Abenazar**: "Speak!" He throws sand on the fire (Page 1)
Thunder

Cue 3 **Voice**: "Now leave me!" (Page 1)
Thunder

Cue 4 As SCENE 9 begins (Page 29)
Early morning sounds

Cue 5 **Abenazar** and **Aladdin** arrive at the mountainous spot (Page 32)
Thin wind

Cue 6 **Abenazar** lights twigs (Page 32)
Smoke from twigs, rumbling sound growing louder, stones fall from pile; continue under dialogue

Cue 7 **Abenazar**: " No, no, just wait." (Page 32)
Rumbling continues; more stones fall from the pile

Cue 8 **Abenazar**: "Keep going, my son!" (Page 34)
Wind rises

Cue 9 **Abenazar**: " ... lock him in forever!" (Page 35)
Thunder

ACT II

Cue 10 The Lights fade (Page 38)
Thunder; mist pours down

Cue 11 **Genie of the Lamp**: "I am the Geni of the Lamp." (Page 38)
Thunder

Cue 11	**Genie of the Lamp**: "To hear is to obey." *Thunder*	(Page 39)
Cue 13	**Genie of the Ring**: " ... when you need me." *Enormous wind sounds*	(Page 39)
Cue 14	**Sung Din**: "... pop out and ..." *Thunder: one clap, then continuous rumble. Mist pours from kitchen*	(Page 40)
Cue 15	**Genie of the Ring**: "Toodleoo." *Flash*	(Page 41)
Cue 16	**Aladdin** rubs the lamp *Thunder; mist*	(Page 60)
Cue 17	**Princess**: "No!" *Crash, flash, cloud of smoke*	(Page 62)
Cue 18	**Rowloon**: "Help!" *Crash, flash*	(Page 62)
Cue 19	**Sung Din**: " ... is in that lamp." *Faint rumble*	(Page 68)
Cue 20	**Princess**: "I really don't know what you're ——" *Thunder, crashes, bangs and whistling sounds, fading*	(Page 68)
Cue 21	**Aladdin** rubs the ring *Flash*	(Page 71)
Cue 22	As Scene 10 begins *Cicadas hum throughout scene*	(Page 73)
Cue 23	**Sung Din**: " ... to hold umbrellas —— " *Roll of thunder*	(Page 76)
Cue 24	**Princess** throws lamp through Genie's mouth *Magical noises*	(Page 76)